WHITE TRASH ETIQUETTE

DR. VERNE EDSTROM, ESQ.

BROADWAY BOOKS • NEW YORK

Broadway Books titles may be purchased for business or promotional use or for special sales. For information, please write to: Special Markets Department, Random House, Inc., 1745 Broadway, New York, NY 10019.

PRINTED IN THE UNITED STATES OF AMERICA

BROADWAY BOOKS and its logo, a letter B bisected on the diagonal, are trademarks of Random House, Inc.

Visit our Web site at www.broadwaybooks.com

First Edition

Library of Congress Cataloging-in-Publication Data
Edstrom, Verne.
[Dr. Verne's Northern white trash etiquette]
White trash etiquette / Verne Edstrom.
p. cm.
Rev. ed. of : Dr. Verne's Northern white trash etiquette. c1999.
1. Rednecks—Middle West—Humor. 2. Working class whites—
Middle West—Humor. I. Title.

PN6231.R38E37 2006
818'.602—dc22   2005050160

ISBN 0-7679-2207-7

3 5 7 9 10 8 6 4

To my beloved wife Toni,

who's prettier than a shot of Jim Beam after you

just hijacked a truckload of patio furniture

CONTENTS

MEET DR. VERNE

ow do?

The name's Dr. Verne Edstrom, Esq. This here's my book.

Now you're probably wondering how wholesome White Trash like me got to be a famous book author, hanging around Deep Literary Guys who don't even own tool belts.

Since you asked, this here's the story:

I was born in St. Cloud, Minnesota, which is over by Wisconsin and Canada. Like most decent trash, I got me a good upbringing.

My ma worked at the quarry and had a sweet AFDC scam going on the side, which taught me good finance at an early age. The old man, he had a union job for about three months when I was six. But mostly he burglarized chicken farms so he could pickle the eggs and sell 'em to bars.

He was a good earner and a good father—until he got shot by Mr. Johansson, who was our neighbor, who wasn't partial to the old man playing hide the power tool with Mrs. Johansson while he was out spearfishing.

The family estate was the envy of St. Cloud. We had a double-wide on 40 acres and more refrigerators on our porch than anybody in town. Some folks might say we was well-to-do.

That's how I got me this prestigious education. I graduated third in my class at the Red Wing Boys Reformatory, which people from them parts will tell you is the Harvard of the Minnesota juvenile correctional system. I also attended the Stillwater State Prison, where I majored in pipefitting.

My first wedding was to Alice. I met her one day while I was robbing a Denny's. You never seen a woman look finer emptying a cash register. Her great big hair was glistening like a clump of jewels. I figured it might be worth something at the pawnshop. Problem is, I couldn't get it unattached from her head.

As it turns out, me and Alice got to sparking and next thing you know we's married with four or six kids—I can't remember which.

But then Alice run off with my brother Hal, who only got one ear cuz the other got bit off by a northern pike in an ice fishing accident. I figured Alice felt sorry for him. That's why I only tried to shoot Hal once.

Then I got married to Karicia, who got a bad name but

a good body. She was what you call your performing artist. Guys still remember her show over at the Palomino Club. She could do some amazing things with a plate of mixed vegetables.

Karicia wasn't partial to having no kids, which is why we only ended up with three. But then I caught her with this guy Sammy in the Palomino men's room. I was pissed, seeing as how he wasn't even kin. So I smacked Sammy with a towel dispenser.

Well, the blood got to flowing and Karicia got to squealing like a lawyer with a scraped knee. So I went home, grabbed the young ones, and headed for Milwaukee. Which is in Wisconsin. Which is where guys is known to wear big globs of cheese on their head. Which is why I figured the law wouldn't catch me. You never seen no cheese police busting nobody on *Cops*, am I right?

Milwaukee's a fine place to raise kids. There ain't no jobs, which means you can stay on unemployment without them social workers squawking at you. It also got a lot of good places to rob, since most people got power tools.

Me and the kids, we was living in paradise.

The Second Foreword

(ON ACCOUNT OF WE COULDN'T AFFORD ALL THE FIRST SO WE HAD TO PUT THIS ONE ON LAYAWAY)

Anyways, I raised them kids right. Taught 'em all my worldly knowledge, like how to hotwire snowmobiles and poach deer.

By junior high, they already had their own scam selling my used *Hustlers* to fifth graders for fifteen bucks a pop. You might say they was born entrepreneurs.

But then I got to figuring the kids needed one of them feminine presences around, someone to teach 'em the fineries of life, like how to cook a decent potpie. So I got hitched to Marci.

If a guy was being charitable, you could say Marci is a fine-looking woman—kind of a female John Goodman, only with more facial hair.

But me being the sensitive kind, I can say with a true heart that it wasn't looks I was after.

Nope, I first got to sparking with Marci when I seen her win the wood-splitting contest at Lumberjack Days. She had the muscles of a beer truck driver. Which meant I could branch out into stealing sofas, on account of them hide-a-beds is damn heavy, so you need a partner with decent pipes.

Marci was a Christian woman. She never used the Lord's name in vain unless she was drunk or shot herself with a nail gun. But she wasn't partial to my thieving ways.

So we up and moved to St. Paul, Minnesota, where the jobs was good. I got me work handling cargo at the airport.

It wasn't a bad job—outside of the actual work. I was making union money and got free steel-tocs. It was also good for stealing luggage. (If there's anybody out there needing a set of them Corinthian leather Samsonites with the fruity wheels on the bottom, give me a call. Everything's priced to move.)

But like most decent trash, me and jobs ain't a good mix. I got what you call disillusioned, which is fancy talk for saying the job sucked. I wanted more from life than stealing suitcases and sleeping in cargo holds. I wanted some of that enrichment and reward, like they's always talking about on infomercials.

So I did what any God-fearing White Trash would do: I faked a back injury.

Soon I was dipping my beak in that sweet nectar of workers' comp. I convinced the old lady we should move to Green Bay, where the fishing was better and the insurance guys wouldn't try to videotape me a butchering moose when I was supposed to be laid up.

But like they say in them Hallmark cards, "Life has a way of ramming a shiv in your neck sometimes." Next thing you know, them pointy-heads from the state says I gotta join one of them retraining programs.

So I got to enrolling in the White Trash Studies program at University of Wisconsin Green Bay, known by academias as one of the finest colleges that got a hyphen in its name. Eleven years later, out comes Dr. Verne Edstrom, Esq.

Now most folks ain't never seen no White Trash doctor—especially one who got a Esq. on top of it. You might say I was a celebrity. Pretty soon, people was coming from near and far to get answers on all their important questions—like what's the classiest whisky for bringing to a job interview, or how to rob a SuperAmerica when you done lost your gun. I got to feelin' so good about helping people out, I decided to start posting my helpful advice where everyone in town could see it so's they could all learn a little bit of class. Which is why I hung the letters up at the racetrack. Pretty soon, people started readin' 'em and writing more letters back. I started getting letters from all over the country. I was like Dr. Phil, only you could trust what I got to say, on account of I didn't wear no candy-assed suit.

Problem is, Marci ain't the kind to impress easy. I hate speaking ill of the woman, but she was putting on airs. If I was such a celebrity, she got to saying, why was we still living in a shack behind the post office?

I tried explaining all the scientific advantages to the family estate—like the fact that it had a sunroof, on account of the part over the kitchen done collapsed in a blizzard.

But Marci can be real persuasive, especially when she uses a busted hockey stick to make her point. By the time I got outta the hospital, I was seeing things her way. So's I gathered up the brood and says, "Brood, we're going to the homeland of our people, the Paris of the White Trash Nation, Cleveland, Ohio."

I was fixing to become a world-famous author.

Now most folks know Cleveland is your epicenter of the White Trash literary scene, on account of it got lots of abandoned buildings, so's a guy could shack up in some solitude while contemplating his latest works. I figured since I was already giving people my scientific advice for free, I'd just make up some new crap and turn 'er into a book. It's what you call your valuable public service.

See, most of your self-help these days gets written up by dainty guys who's always squawking about their saturated fat. But there wasn't no self-help for decent trash.

Say you got an important question, like how to make your fourteen-year-old cousin unpregnant, or who you should kidnap if you're aiming to impress a woman. You think you're gonna ask Dr. Laura about that? Her face would explode and her makeup would catch fire. Pretty soon you burned down eleven states, but you still don't know who you're supposed to abduct.

Me, I was figuring to help folks rise up from under the viaduct—teach 'em a little etiquette, help 'em get a little class—so they could do better robberies, get themselves more marriages, and start living the life of luxury in a nice double-wide where the heat always works and the cupboards is always filled with liquor and ammo.

You might say I was just giving something back to the community.

And if you ain't buying that explanation, here's a better one: I got eight or ten kids. Seeing as how Marci's built like them ore boats on the Cuyahoga River, the smart money says she's good for a half-dozen more. So if you don't buy my book, I don't get no money, which means eight to ten kids is gonna be loose on the streets, stealing your car stereo.

And any moron knows a book is cheaper than a car stereo. That's just good financial thinking.

Dr. Verne Edstrom, Esq.
Cleveland, America

Acknowledgments

Special thanks to my editor at Broadway, Beth Datlowe Adams, who plucked my ass outta obscurity, and don't even make me pay rent to sleep in her car. I'd also like to thank my agent, but I don't got one on account of I fired him, 'cause he didn't buy me no whiskey. What's the point of having an agent if he don't kiss your ass? Most important, I'd like to thank all the little people I stepped on to get famous. (No, kid, you ain't getting your bike back. If you want a bike, steal one like a decent American.)

Author's Note

All letters in this book is real. Some locations got changed
to protect the writers from bill collectors, parole officers,
ex-husbands, and the guy whose Lynyrd Skynyrd 8-track
they borrowed and never brought back

WHITE
TRASH
ETIQUETTE

Introduction

HOW TO KNOW IF YOU'RE DECENT TRASH

What you're looking at is one of them scientific tests, invented by authentic pointy-heads with lab coats, so you know it's good. It's designed to see if you're decent trash—which means you're worthy of finding out my patented system for success—or if you're some kinda lowlife, like a congressman or a CEO, who we don't want polluting this book.

Check your score at the end. If you gotta get somebody to read it for you, add two points.

1. **What makes you and your old man fight the most?**
   A. When you catch him tomcatting with the lady from apartment 314, who got a better mustache than Tom Selleck.

   B. When he leaves the toilet seat up, and the kids start using it as a swimming pool.

   C. When he forgets to tape the strongman competition on ESPN while you're working the graveyard shift.

2. **Yuppies is good for:**
   A. Charging $17,000 for a new tranny on their Acura, on account of they don't know better.
   B. Chopping up and selling for bait on the pier.
   C. When you run out of clay pigeons.

3. **What's the most important thing to teach your kids?**
   A. How to read so they can understand the racing form.
   B. Chemistry, just in case they need to make pipe bombs sometime.
   C. Math. Cuz that's the lie you always use during parent-teacher conferences.

4. **What's the most important thing to look for in a fourth husband?**
   A. He's gotta be good in bed, so you'll have something to do when the TV gets repossessed.
   B. He's gotta have a job, or at least a good personal injury case going.
   C. He's gotta be handy with a nail gun, just in case your bookie comes around looking for the money you owe him.

5. **What's the most important thing to look for in a fourth wife?**

   A. She's gotta know not to talk when the Bengals is on.

   B. Her butt's gotta be small enough to fit in a movie theater seat.

   C. She's gotta be good at lying to the bill collectors, on account of you shouldn't have to do all the damn work around here.

6. **Which old country did your ancestors came from?**

   A. Greece

   B. Newark.

   C. The Greyhound terminal.

7. **Your kid takes a small helping for supper. What do you do?**

   A. Question his sexual preference.

   B. Search his room to see if he's buying cologne, too.

   C. Tell him to eat up, on account of you ain't raising him to be no supermodel

8. **If you was to win a free vacation from the door-to-door vacuum cleaner salesman, and you could go anywhere, which place would you get your ass to?**

   A. Germany, cuz they got a good supply of beer.

   B. Palm Springs, cuz there's lots of old rich people who's easy to mug.

C. Vegas, cuz the old lady loves that Wayne Newton, which means she'll cut you some slack next time she catches you with her sister behind the Dumpster.

9. **Say one of your trees falls on the neighbor's property. You and him got a beef over who should clean it up. What do you do?**
   A. Forget about it. He never used the part of his house that got crushed anyways.
   B. Shoot him. It ain't polite manners that he's bothering you during the TNT Clint Eastwood marathon.
   C. Tell him he owes you $200, on account of that tree's worth a lotta lumber, then sue 'im when he don't pay.

10. **You get a call from the school counselor. Your kid got in a fight. Your first response is:**
    A. "Unless you can prove the kid's mine, quit calling."
    B. "You wanna buy some night crawlers?"
    C. "Don't worry. He's just coming down from a meth bender."

11. **Your sixteen-year-old daughter tells you she's pregnant. What do you do?**
    A. Tell her it's about time.
    B. Do the loving parent thing and let her put it on your tab at Planned Parenthood.

C. Tell her she's gotta move out. She's an adult now and should get her own damned AFDC scam.

12. You just won the lottery. What do you do?

  A. Hire one of them pointy-heads with the cute little glasses to invest it wisely.

  B. Pay off your delinquent child support, which'll leave enough money left for a carton of Winstons.

  C. Blow it on slot machines, Jim Beam, and chicken.

13. You just got sentenced to eighteen months for your third drunk driving. Now is a good time to:

  A. Stab somebody, on account of the food ain't bad here and you'll get to stay longer.

  B. Turn your life over to God. Maybe He'll pay your lawyer bill.

  C. Sweet-talk that lady guard. She's making union money and probably got a nice house with shag carpet and them matador paintings. It'd be a good place for laying on the couch once you get paroled.

14. You're out on your first date with the cute guy from the loading dock. He asks what you want to drink. What do you do?

  A. Order one of them top-shelf liqueurs. A man's attractiveness is directly related to how much loot he's willing to blow on you.

B. Only order a double-shot of Wild Turkey, cuz you wanna seem ladylike.

C. Order Diet Pepsi. It'll be easier to get yourself knocked up if he don't think you're gonna turn into John Madden once you get hitched.

15. The landlord calls about the rent being late. Pick the proper White Trash response:

A. "My deepest apologies. I will inform the trust fund administrator at once."

B. "Aw, $#@&. My mailman musta got cut down in one of them postal shootings again."

C. "What &%$#@$#% rent check? I paid you cash two months ago when I hit on the Fireball machine at the Indian casino! Are you trying to %$#@ me here? I got witnesses, mother%$#@$%! You want a piece of me?"

16. If you could shack up with any movie star, who would it be?

A. Burt Reynolds, on account of you lost your dishrag, and his wig would make a good replacement.

B. Hugh Grant. He talks funny. Your kids could take him to Show and Tell.

C. Robert Duvall, on account of he's handsome like Steve Buscemi, but he played a Mafia guy in *The Godfather*, so he could probably get you a five-finger discount on a camcorder.

17. **You're short on jack for Christmas. What's the best way to score quick cash?**
   A. Mug a FedEx guy. You might score something big, like the payroll checks from an International House of Pancakes.
   B. Rob a deli. You ain't done one for a couple weeks, and the Job Corps counselor is always saying how you should keep your skills fresh.
   C. Rob a veterinarian. The kids always wanted a half-pound of horse tranquilizers for Christmas.

18. **You dug a septic tank for this guy from work last summer, but he ain't paid up. What's the proper White Trash way for handling the situation?**
   A. Set his house on fire, but don't forget to bring the marshmallows.
   B. Let your dog chew on him, on account of he's cheaper than Purina.
   C. Offer to trade the unpaid bill for that seventy-eight-pound sturgeon he got mounted on his wall. It'll make for good bragging when the in-laws come over.

19. **It's you and your woman's tenth anniversary (if you don't count the time she was shacking up with that trucker from Indiana). You wanna do something classy. What's your best move?**
   A. Give her your leftover KFC from lunch.

B. Steal some flowers from a rich lady's lawn, then have your buddy deliver 'em so it looks like you paid top dollar.

C. Make her a nice Swanson's dinner and put on the Pirates game, then let her sit in the good recliner tonight—just so she don't make a habit of it.

20. **It's Saturday night. Your old man's got the annual Ducks Unlimited banquet. But you're playing third base for Len's Bar in the state softball regionals. Problem is, you got no babysitter. What do you do?**

A. Make the old man take 'em to the banquet. The kids gotta learn to drink sometime.

B. Let 'em stay home by themselves. This is what shrinks call nurturing their independence.

C. Put 'em in foster care. Your folks did it to you, and you ain't turned out so bad.

Correct Answers:

This here's the answers. Count up the number you got right.

1. A	8. C	15. C
2. B	9. A	16. A
3. B	10. C	17. B
4. C	11. C	18. A
5. B	12. C	19. B
6. C	13. A	20. A
7. B	14. B	

If you can't count, get your kids to do it—that's what you send 'em to school for. And if your kids got sent to juvie hall, just make your score up. It ain't like your probation officer is watching.

Find Your White Trash Rating

Now that you got to calculating up your score, use this here chart to see if you's decent or scum. This'll clue you in on how much work you got to reach your full White Trash potential.

17–20: A

You're authentic trash. You probably hit a ton of homers in softball and guys is always asking you to join their dart team. Stick with me, pal, and you'll own your own chop shop someday.

13–16: B

You're pretty good trash, but you turned a little fruity after putting designer mustard on your ballpark dog that one time. I ain't saying you're cut out for trash royalty, but if you read this book, you could probably be a foreman and make some good side money stealing plywood from the warehouse. And if anybody tries to give you some designer mustard again, hit 'im in the face with a snow shovel. He's probably from France.

8–12: C

You're a half-breed: part trash, part yuppie. You're probably handy with a power auger, but your last brawl was in junior high, when you got your ass kicked by a guy named Chad. Don't worry. There's still hope.

If you follow my scientific teachings, keep your mouth shut, and quit reading that goddamned *Men's Health*, you could probably get into the Teamsters. Me and you could do some nice truck hijackings together if you bring the beer.

4–7: D

You got a man-purse. You probably go rollerblading in spandex. And what the hell's up with all them David Spade posters you got hanging in your garage? I'm thinking you need an intervention. Read this book seven times then give me a call. For the sake of your kin, I'm willing to do some private tutoring so long as you buy the shots and we don't gotta watch no fruity PAC-10 football on the bar TV.

1–3: F

God don't like you. That's why He got you a job in banking. Figure yourself lucky that He ain't had your ass eaten by locusts yet.

If you was to try burglarizing a construction site, you'd probably drop a concrete block on your foot. The shrieking would blow up the pacemakers in grandmas for miles around. So quit your bawling and start reading the book, grandma killer. At least it'll keep you outta trouble.

(In case you's
wondering, this ain't
Chapter 1. This here's
your Roman
numerals, which was
thought up by them
ancient Romanians.
Everybody knows
these guys was
deep—even if they
pranced around in
bedsheets on account
of nobody invented
clothes yet.)

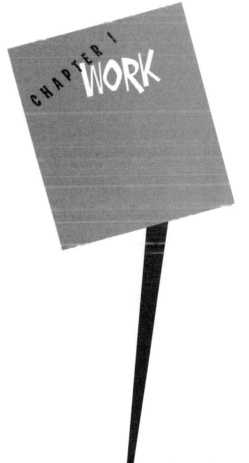

CHAPTER 1
WORK

Now unless you wanna spend your golden years like your grandma—living in a Pontiac in the scrap yard—decent trash knows they gotta earn so you always got money for cigs and meat. But a lot of people has a hard time figuring out what's the best career option: work, welfare, workers' comp, or crime?

Most folks go straight to welfare or workers' comp, seeing as how jobs and crime can rarely compete with laying on the couch all day watching cable. You don't wanna be stuck cleaning bathrooms or casing out a laundromat if some fat lady's gonna take off her shirt on *Jerry Springer* today, am I right?

But unless you got a job sewing Nikes in China, working generally pays better than welfare, which means you got more jack to buy them fineries in life, like Hamburger Helper and propane. And the fact is, some jobs ain't all bad.

How to Tell If Your Job Sucks

In its recent scientifical report entitled *Jobs That Don't Suck*, the U.S. Department of Commerce discovered there were at least thirteen in America.

So how do you know if you got one of 'em? Just answer yes or no to the following questions. Your job's suckage rating got figured at the bottom.

1. Does your job got free coffee that ain't that limp-wristed kind guys with berets and sandals drink?

2. Can you ash on the floor and set fire to stuff if nobody's using it?

3. Do you get time off on major holidays, like Opening Day, St. Patrick's, and Deer Hunting Season?

4. Is it okay to be drunk some of the time, just so it ain't every day?

5. Do the other employees bring good lunches you can steal outta the company fridge when they ain't looking?

6. Does the boss still fall for the Call-in-a-Bomb-Threat-When-You's-Too-Hung-Over-to-Show-Up-for-Work Scam?

7a. If you're a man, do the women employees wear halter tops and not look like them Russian ladies?

7b. If you're a woman, are the men employees you're having affairs with respectful enough not to call your house when the old man's home?

8. Is there wildlife you can shoot out the window during lunchtime?

9. Is there a bitchy human resource lady who's fun to torture by putting cig burns in her paperwork and telling her, "You look pretty today, kinda like Eva Braun"?

10. Can you make a decent score by busting into the pop machine when no one's looking?

Suckage Rating

Give yourself 1 point for each yes answer.

- **8–10:** If you answered yes to eight or more questions, you're probably in the Lucky Thirteen. That means it ain't a good idea to spray paint cars in the executive parking lot no more.
- **5–7:** Your job's probably worth keeping—if you answered yes to question 10 and you're getting at least fifty bucks a week.
- **3–4:** Get your ass outta there right quick—but don't forget to hold up the payroll department before you leave!
- **0–2:** What are you, some kind of moron?

The Ten Hottest White Trash Career Opportunities

Now I'm figuring most of you done failed that last test. That's because the guys who invented jobs is called "bosses," which is Cherokee for "Antichrist." But don't go a worrying. Your ol' pal Verne got you covered.

Fact is, ever since them bulletproof windows killed the convenience store robbing industry, it ain't been easy for people to score themselves a decent career. And seeing how most of the factory jobs gone to China and Mississippi, where the bus line don't go, a lot of us trash is in what you call your state of despair.

But there's still a lot of jobs where you hardly have to work—much less show up—and the pay's better than AFDC.

According to my scientific calculations, this here's gonna be the Top Ten White Trash growth professions in the twenty-first century. So stop looking at the *Baywatch* reruns and pay attention.

1. CEO

The upside:

The hardest thing you're ever gonna do is say, "Have my helicopter ready in ten minutes, Cheeves." Most of the time you sit around pretending to read reports from the Pacific Rim project or firing people cuz they're too old. And you always got an excuse for missing work when you get drunk and fall off the porch. Just call your secretary and say, "I'll be at home working on my vision statement today." Nobody ever actually reads these things, so nobody's gonna know you was actually watching Judge Judy, who's kinda hot for an old broad.

The downside:

Guys'll expect you to play golf, which means you gotta dress up like retirees from Florida and swing little clubs that ain't even manly enough to hunt gooses with.

You also gotta get one of them molded executive hairdos, which means hacking off the mullet. Forget about ever shacking up again with ladies who can hold decent conversations about muscle cars.

The pay:
Higher than you can count with an eighth-grade public school education. Plus, you get stock options. I don't exactly know what these is, but you ever see a CEO mooching drinks at closing time?

2. Crack Whore

The upside:
You can call in sick every day on account of it's part of the job requirements. You don't gotta pay taxes or rent, cuz crack whores figure good living is clean cardboard in an alley behind a carpet store. Plus, you get to travel to exotic places like the bus station.

The downside:
No paid vacations. Company headquarters is the men's room of a Phillips 66.

The pay:
None. But since you're keeping expenses low, this is what them granola eaters call living off the fat of the land.

3. Designated Hitter

The upside:
Sit on the bench, say uplifting things like, "C'mon,

Jonesy, we need a hit," swing a bat four times a day, then beeline it to the clubhouse deli spread before your teammates get in and all that's left is the bean salad.

The downside:
You don't get to play in the field. That means you won't score extra bus fare when the drunks pelt you with quarters in Detroit.

The pay:
We're talking guaranteed contracts of $5 million a year, plus you get to gouge kids twenty bucks a pop for autographing their crap at card shows.

4. Trophy Wife
The upside:
Watch TV. Lunch. Watch more TV.

The downside:
You gotta marry some candy-ass who'll buy you exercise equipment, which means if you pound cheese puffs all day, he'll trade you in for a new model that runs on grapefruit and bean sprouts.

The pay:
Free Lexus, big screen, and makeup. You also get unlimited credit cards to binge shop for halter tops and plastic lawn animals.

5. Third World Dictator

The upside:

You can call yourself a general and order aircraft carriers to take your buddies fishing. Live in a palace where they got servants who'll fetch cigs and chocolate milk from the Circle K.

The downside:

Everybody's calling you El Presidente, which sounds kinda sissified for the boss of a country. Most third world gas stations ain't worth robbing. Everybody talks Mexican on cable.

The pay:

You own the country. This comes in handy when you're short on gas money.

6. Symphony Violinist

The upside:

Hack away with a funny stick on a violin, then pretend the screeching is famous music from Austria. Rich guys pay top dollar to hear this stuff. You only gotta work three-hour shifts. And the boss is some guy who wears white gloves and is always flopping his arms like a mallard with a sore wing, which means you don't gotta follow his orders. What's he gonna do to you? Hit you with his little baton?

The downside:

You gotta wear a tux. Your relatives is gonna think you're a waiter from them bird food restaurants downtown.

The pay:

How am I supposed to know? Get off your ass and find out yourself. I'm tired of doing all the work here.

7. Bar Hag

The upside:

Sit at the bar, sweet-talk toothless guys who couldn't buy a decent woman with a profit sharing check, and be ugly.

The downside:

Shifts last from 6:00 a.m. to 2:00 a.m. You gotta survive on cocktail wieners from happy hour.

The pay:

Free drinks. Some nights you get to sleep in the cab of a new Dodge Ram.

8. Congressman

The upside:

Basically the same job as a bar hag: sit around, blab, and mooch stuff. Mostly you just eat free steak dinners from lobbyists, go on fact-finding missions to country clubs in Hawaii, and vote to let chemical companies build hazardous waste dumps at preschools.

The downside:

They cut out your heart as a job requirement. People will keep a close eye on you so you can't steal the silverware when you come over for dinner.

The pay:

Six figures plus bribes, junkets, free dinners, sex with interns, and an office full of Ivy League ass-kissers who can haul shingles in case you get a roofing job.

9. Punk Rock Hairdresser

The upside:

Change your name to François, get a caulking gun, blast their hair with some tub and tile sealer, mess it all up, and charge 'em $100 a pop. They're punkers. They'll think it's cutting edge.

The downside:

You gotta tell people you're a hairdresser. If you get the urge to color coordinate your belt and your shoes, call 911.

The pay:

One hundred bucks for three minutes of work. Try making that selling plasma.

10. Workers' Comp

The upside:

It's kind of like being a trophy wife, only without the credit cards or exercise equipment. Just fake a back injury, sit around reading *TV Digest*, watch fishing shows, and have your kids fetch you Rolling Rock and Count Chocula.

The downside:
You gotta go to the doctor. Sometimes they schedule appointments in the middle of that Bruins–Islanders replay you was meaning to watch.

The pay:
Four hundred dollars a month, plus quality time with the kids in front of the TV.

How to Show Class and Not Get Shot While You're Robbing the 7-Eleven

Yeah, yeah, I hear you. Right about now you're saying to yourself, "Hey, Verne, if robbing convenience stores was good enough for my ma, why can't I carry on the family business?"

Now ol' Verne ain't against following in the footsteps of our ancestors. Hell, if it wasn't for them giving us a proper raising, we'd probably growed up to be like them candy-asses on *The Surreal Life* or CNN.

But us trash got a problem: Since our folks mostly run off with the neighbor lady or joined the enriching ranks of the professional bar hag industry, there ain't no one around to sermonize on the sacred teachings these days. Which means a lotta your younger trash ain't clued in on the finer points of thieving.

People is always getting shot. They're trying to rob the BP but ending up at the Mailbox Express by mistake. And half of 'em can't even remember to grab them baby formulas and Newports the old lady was wanting.

Now these ain't the kinda job skills a guy could learn at the orphanage. It don't take no ironworkers apprentice program degree to tell you them nuns ain't exactly earned their journeyman's when it comes to sticking up a Tank 'n' Tummy.

Which is why I got to calculating this scientific checklist. If we're gonna carry on the sacred traditions, we at least gotta get some of them professionalisms, show a little class. You don't wanna put in a hard day's robbing, and all you got to show for it is a pack of teriyaki jerky and three bullets in your face, am I right?

Picking a Good Place to Rob

The first question when it comes to choosing your mark is, "Is it open?" Robbing, in case you ain't noticed, ain't particularly easy when the store is closed.

This here happened to my sister Jenny. Her fifth husband got killed when he broke into the zoo and tried to rob the lion cage. Since them lions looked like they was eating good, he figured they musta had a meat supply worth stealing.

Which meant that Jenny had to take over the family business. So she figured she'd do a 4:00 a.m. job at the 7-Eleven, on account of all they had on Bravo was them goddamned celebrity poker shows.

Now a lot of guys is partial to early morning robbing. You can go straight to work after closing time, and that's when the fresh donuts gets delivered.

Problem is, Jenny lives in Buffalo, which is up near Canadia, which is colder than a lawyer's heart. And this particular 7-Eleven was only open from 6:00 a.m. to midnight. Which meant that Jenny had to stand around for two hours waiting for the robbery to get started.

She ended up with a pretty good score. Got herself thirty-eight bucks and a baker's dozen of glazed. Me, I woulda gone with the chocolate cream, but this here's what you call your minor professional differences.

Anyways, them two hours of waiting done froze her feet. She got arthritis. The doc says she can't do no more winter robbing.

Now if you was living in Houston, this ain't a problem. But in Buffalo it's always winter except on August 13. Which meant that Jenny had to get a part-time job shoplifting from the Junior Miss section at the Gap. I don't gotta tell you them pawnshops ain't exactly paying top dollar for pleated skorts in mango orange. The family business was ruined.

Choosing the Right Gun

Most of your professional robbers prefer the handgun. Them babies is light and small, which means you can hide 'em under your Phillies hat if you get drunk and forget to wear any pants. Besides, nothing says "I'm here to rob you" better than your handcrafted piece of American steel.

Now other guys is partial to the sawed-off. It comes in two colors, metallic blue and silver, which fashion guys'll tell you is good for accessorizing with your Raiders jersey in case you's doing a job in Oakland.

Still other guys got fondness for the good ol' buck knife. She's cheap, on account of she don't need no ammo. She's also easy carrying if your car got stoled and you gotta walk to the robbery. And if you happen to be strolling home down the freeway and you was to come across a dead possum, that's just bonus round. You can skin her on the spot and score yourself some dinner.

But if you're asking me, there's only one bad boy you wanna show up with at the Diamond Shamrock. I'm talking about the .44 caliber Brass Frame Buffalo Revolver.

This here black powder beauty is what Old West trash used when they was robbing the stagecoach. You know them boys had class, seeing as how they're still showing their robbing highlight films on Turner Classic. And if you was to steal a horse and come riding into the Circle K, all the customers'd be inviting you to rob their place, seeing as how they'd figure you was from the movies.

Just don't eat the horse till after the robbery. They don't ride too good when they're all chewed up.

Best of all, your Buffalo Revolver got a twelve-inch barrel. So if you happen to rob a Kum 'n' Go, and the clerk don't speak English, you could use it as a pointer so he don't mess up your donut order.

I don't gotta tell you that nothing ruins a robbery more than getting home, opening your bag a loot, and finding out you got a dozen garlic bagels instead of them cheese blintzes you was hankering after.

Hood or Ski Mask?

The ski mask used to be your standard gear. Then the Unabomber done busted out that Hood & Sunglasses Look. Seeing as how he was on TV, everyone figured the guy got a ton of chicks. So all the trash started wearing it, too.

Now I ain't saying you got problems with your ski mask. One time I was robbing this store in Flint, Michigan, and the clerk kept asking me for tips on the giant slalom. Since us trash is known for our gentlemanliness, I always make time for a question-and-answer period. Which meant I was late for supper.

But I'm figuring the Hood & Sunglasses Look gives your robbery a mixed message. This guy's called the Unabomber, not the Unarobber. So say you hit a Quik Mart. Problem is, the clerk figures you're there to do a bombing. And since this is usually a one-man job, he thinks you don't need no help, so he punches out and goes home.

That means instead of you getting to wave your gun and boss him around, which is the funnest part of robbing, you gotta do all the work. And avoiding work was the whole reason you got a robbing career in the first place.

Rope or Telephone Cord?

A lot of top robbers like to do the job right quick. Maybe they's taking the old lady to see Kenny Wayne Shepherd that night. Or maybe they just don't wanna leave the kids alone in the car too long, on account of they'll mooch all your cigs.

But other guys like to savor the job, do some of that basking in professional glory. Which means you gotta tie up the victims so's you got time to read *Fins and Feathers*.

In the old days, you could just tie everybody up with a telephone cord. But now everybody got a cell phone. Which means the clerks keep getting loose and calling the cops.

Now ol' Verne got no beef with cops. They's decent working people, and usually got a good supply of power tools if you was to rob their garage.

But cops gotta way of introducing you to judges. And judges gotta way of introducing you to prison. And prison gotta way of introducing you to an eight-foot-tall guy named Harry, who might get to thinking you look pretty, even if half your face got burnt off in an industrial accident.

Which is a long way of saying that you should always bring a telephone to your robbery.

Making Your Hostage Situation Fun for the Whole Family

Everybody knows what to grab first: the seventy-nine bucks from the cash register, a couple packs of Swisher Sweets, and that new Waylon Jennings Christmas CD.

But that's when the selecting gets hard. If you ain't made a shopping list, chances are you're getting stuck when you gotta decide between the *Sports Illustrated* or a bottle of that Valvoline Stop Leak.

This happened to my pal Billy. His selecting got so long the cops surrounded the place. So he got hisself in one of them hostage situations.

This here's where a lot of your younger trash go wrong. Since they ain't been teached on the fineries, they learnt their hostage situating from TV. Which means you're supposed to do a lot of yelling and shooting into the ceiling. Which is a waste of good ammo on account of there ain't usually no ducks up there. Which means your hostages is gonna think you suck at duck hunting. Which means TV robbers got no class.

Seeing as how us trash is prone to gentlemanliocity, you gotta think of your hostage situation like hosting a party.

If you have to herd a batch of schoolkids into the beer cooler, make sure you grab some packs of Bubblicious and have a singalong. I usually go with Raffi or Megadeth. Kids is partial to them guys.

And if you got a batch of adults, crack open the forty-ouncers of Pabst and party on. Anyone who serves free beer is probably gonna have a waiting list for their next hostage situation. But don't let your guests get too hammered. They're gonna start bawling about their old lady leaving 'em, and you won't be able to hear the police negotiators over the phone.

But there's a couple things you wanna avoid: First off, don't do no hostage situations in yuppie neighborhoods.

A buddy of mine, Big Larry, once got lost and robbed a Starbucks by mistake. There wasn't no liquor on hand. Then the hostages wanted to hold a book discussion. Big

Larry had to surrender. He figured it was better than listening to them read that goddamned Maya Angelou anymore.

You also don't wanna start no card game. Chances are one of your hostages might be a shark. Next thing you know, she got the whole seventy-nine bucks you was meaning to take home from the robbery.

And you sure as hell don't wanna play no strip poker. One time I had me a pack of Mary Kay salesladies as hostages. So I figured I'd start a game, take their money, and get to see 'em bare naked to boot. Next thing you know, they done won all my clothes, my gun, and the Dale Earnhardt Jr. hat I was meaning to steal.

I had to take the bus home with only my tube socks on. It wasn't one of the prouder moments in White Trash history.

Your Getaway

Here's the first rule of making your getaway: Do not call a cab.

Say you just robbed a nice batch of Captain Crunch, but like usual, the cab don't show up for two hours. Chances are you forgot to rob some milk. Which means you gotta stand outside the store eating dry cereal while you wait.

Rule number two: If you're gonna use a car, make sure it runs.

I once heard about this one guy in Pensacola, Florida. He was figuring on using his '78 Impala for the getaway. It was Sunday morning. He was gonna nail a string of robberies, then beeline her home in time for the Buccaneers–Falcons game.

Problem is, after his first job at the Minit Mart, his damn car wouldn't start. So by the time he pushed it to the next job, the place had already been robbed. All that was left was a sixer of Genuine Draft. He didn't even get home till the third quarter.

That's why your quality robbers is prone to hiring a licensed driver. While you're busy doing the robbing, he can make sure the radio's turned to your favorite station. Last thing you want is to get caught in a high-speed chase, and you gotta listen to Journey as your soundtrack.

By this point, I figure I got you all clued in on the job situation. But maybe somebody got to reading some of that Maya Angelou around you, and your head still ain't right.

Which is why I got me this question-and-answer period. Just like when you're robbing, the decent self-help guy always makes time for morons who's a little slow on the uptake. So let's go to the mailbag:

Earn Jack and Score Chicks
Through the Lost Art of Kidnapping

Dear Dr. Verne:

I got this problem. They're trying to wussify me.

I had a good job fixin' lawn mowers at Sears. One day me and the boss got to fighting. That was the beginning of my problems.

I lost my job. Now I'm stuck working in some wussy-ass hotel.

I wanted to work at one of them classy places. The place I work for don't even got vibrating beds or PBR at the bar.

I just got word from my friend down in Missouri. He got a brand-new bass boat, a huge house (it's a double-wide) and is about to get hitched with a girl that can tune his truck. How can I compete with this?

—Wussified in Rapid City

Dear Wussified:

Working at a hotel ain't gonna get you the good life of double-wides and bass boats. Women ain't partial to sparking with guys whose main job is to say, "Would you like a nonsmoking room with a view of the stockyards?" I'm guessing you couldn't even afford plastic covers for their good couch.

Which is why you gotta change careers. The way I'm thinking, you need one of them decent careers where the money's good, the hours is short, and most of your time's spent sleeping or doing beer bongs.

I'm talking kidnapping.

Used to be this was a decent trade for us trash. A guy could nab a couple of rich fruities, collect some decent ransom, then retire to one

of them vacation paradises like Dubuque on the fruits of his labor.

I'm figuring a good person to kidnap would be a sanitation worker or a mailman. They both got union jobs that pay over minimum, which means you could probably hold 'em ransom for 135 bucks or more. Think about all the chicks you'll be scoring when you flash that 135 around the bar. That's the kinda sweet jack that says to a lady, "Yeah, I got your electrolysis payments covered."

Which means the chicks will be attacking you like a herd of starved buffaloes. I'm guessing at least one of 'em gotta have a double-wide and a bass boat, even if you do gotta live at her folks.

Why Hockey Is a Better Job Than the Marines

Dear Dr. Verne:

When I was sixteen I dropped out of school so I could get the manliest job I could think of, the U.S. Marine Corps. It was great. They gave me a gun and let me shoot pinko commie bastards for a living. Then on the weekend (when I wasn't kicking butt), me and the boys would go down to Tijuana, get loaded off tequila, beat the &%$# out of some Navy boys, and score us some women.

Nowadays, I'm lucky if I get to kick ass once a month, seeing as all we do is "peacekeeping" mis-

sions and fighting Arabs, which ain't even com-
mies, and they been givin' me wussy paper-pushin'
jobs. What's worse is now they lettin' in women
and fruity Zima-drinkin' boys who couldn't load a
tow missile if their life depended on it.

I was thinkin' of leaving and joining a militia,
but I don't want to leave my old Corps. What
should I do?

—Corps Forever

Dear Corps:
First thing you gotta do is get a new name. I'm
figuring your ma musta been drunk when she
give birth, cuz most right-thinking trash don't
name their kid after a dead guy laying in the
street.

But I'm feeling for you on this Marines
thing. Fact is, they's getting unmanlified. It
used to be that decent people like you could
make a good living shooting commies, getting
hammered, and smacking around them Navy
fruits. But you don't wanna join no militia.

Militias is like the army of Idaho, which ain't
even a country. They're too cheap to even have
a president or money with pictures of Idaho
guys on it.

Besides, them militias is partial to Hitler,
who was this guy whose ass we kicked back in
the old days, before they invented color and
the world was in black and white. He had a

really bad mustache. Which means militia guys only get the leftover chicks, like them babes on *Sex and the City*, who probably can't even hang drywall.

If you's looking for the pursuit of manly adventure, there's only one line of work for you: hockey player.

They got a job called goon. You only gotta play five minutes a game, punch somebody out, then go sit down again. It's even better than being a bouncer, cuz there's no college boys playing rap on the jukebox.

A few years back, they started letting Ruskies into the league on account of affirmative action. You can hack 'em with your stick all you want. That's only a two-minute penalty.

Now I'm asking you, Corps, where else can you get a job that offers free lumber, laundry, and dental, you get a clubhouse with decent carpeting, and no one calls your parole officer when you brawl?

Plus, in hockey you get to keep your mullet, so's you don't gotta get one of them bad Marines hairdos that only gets you them *Sex and the City* chicks.

If It Got French in It, It Ain't a Manly Job

Dear Dr. Verne:

I been reading your advice for some time now.

Most times I agree with you, but you keep talking about hockey being a manly job.

I got news for you, Verne: The only people who's good at hockey is pussy foreigners like French Canadians, Norwegias, and Minnesotans. In case you don't know, French Canadians got their ass kicked outta Louisiana, where even the deers is midgets. Which means when you stuff 'em and hang 'em above the TV, people think you got a big clump of dog fur glued on the wall.

The only manly thing to come from Minnesota is the women. And if anybodies with names like Ole, Udder, Sven, or Idder shows up at the trailer park, they gets beat up outta what we call principle.

So unless you're from French Canadia or something, I suggest you stop calling someone on ice skates who talks like he got beer foam coming outta his nose a manly type, cause he ain't.

—Buford in Des Moines

Dear Buford:

I can tell you're worldly, seeing as how you got knowledge on foreign places like Canadia. You also got it right about anything French being at least part fruity, on account of they invented hairspray.

But you got it all wrong about Canadia.

For your info, Canadia is the Mecca of the White Trash. Wouldn't you wanna live where the government pays you to eat donuts, shoot

caribou, and pass out on the highway? It's true. I heard it on TV.

Now a lotta guys think Canadia is sissified on account of they never get in no decent wars. But my cousin Elmer, he lives in Winnipeg, and he says it's candy-ass to shoot somebody with a tank. Real men, they strap on the skates, grab some sticks, and see who can gut the other guy like a twelve-point buck, man-to-man.

I ain't agreeing with you on Minnesota either, seeing as how even the women grow beards in the winter, is good at fishing, and can hold their liquor. Plus, they got all them Swedes who ain't too smart, so's it's easy to sneak out on your bar tab.

But I'm kinda agreeing with you on them Norwegias. That's over by Europe, where they's always eating bran flakes and flicking their ponytails like supermodels. But for your info, the Norwegias suck at hockey. Their main job is climbing up the side of a mountain in leather shorts so they can do some yodeling, which sounds kinda like singing after you got your knee cut off in a bandsaw accident.

And I don't gotta tell you that yelping on a mountain ain't a very good job, on account of there ain't no Pepsi machine to rob at lunchtime.

**(Don't be ascared.
We're gonna talk
about gambling and
beating up
stockbrokers.)**

CHAPTER 11

MONEY AND
FINANCE

Ever since the Vikings landed in Ireland and told 'em they was just looking for a decent pancake house, the White Trash has been the world's best liars. You might say it's a gift from God, on account of He got guilt for shorting us when He was passing out the teeth.

Fact is, all the greatest lies in history—"The check is in the mail," "I coulda sworn she was eighteen," and "I'm an innocent man, you honor"—was thought up by us trash. If we was to go to law school, they'd probably put us in the gifted class.

This comes in handy when you're practicing the most important part of high finance.

How to Scam Outta Your Gambling Debts

After all, gambling involves taking on the three most powerful forces in the Universe: your woman, your boss, and your bookie.

Let's start with the baddest, the one who can do you the most damage: your woman.

This is where a lotta guys go wrong. They get to figuring, "Hey, I'm the man. I'm the breadwinner around here. If I wanna drop fifty bucks on the Wolverines, I'm gonna. A man's gotta be the king of his own row house, otherwise what's the point of having chest hairs?"

But this here's what pointy-headed college guys call your "delusional thinking," which is fancy talk for saying you're a dumb ass.

Everybody knows women run the world. Sure, men get all the good jobs, like president and foreman. But women got the power.

Take the president. Say he wants to bomb South Carolina, on account of he's slumping in the polls. But say his woman don't want him to, on account of she don't wanna see no blown up people on TV unless it's a movie or foreigners.

If he goes ahead and bombs, she ain't making him supper. Which means he's gotta eat them convenience store subs with the ham that looks like it was butchered in 1973.

That's why you can't be talking about no breadwinner

stuff. You gotta finesse the situation. And "finesse" is Chippewa for "lying your ass off."

Let's try ourselves a pop quiz.

Say your woman lets you keep a hundred bucks outta each paycheck for everyday stuff, like cigs and gas and crank. But say you lay fifty bucks on the Thrashers over San Jose.

First off, what the hell you betting on the Thrashers for? A course you're gonna lose. Which means you'll run out of money before the next payday. Which means you gotta ask your woman for more.

Do you:

A. Tell her you bet on the Thrashers and lost again?

B. Tell her you was robbed, but the guy only took $55 (don't forget the juice) cuz he didn't want to be stealing too much from no family man?

C. Tell her you happen to run into Father McGarry, and he was saying how they need money for the parish horseshoe league, so you donated $55?

D. All of the above.

If you answered A, you're about to get your ass kicked. Even your woman knows not to bet on the Thrashers.

If you answered B, you suck at lying. Either quit betting or get divorced.

If you answered D, you're good at talking outta your ass. You'd make a good drunk or a senator from Mississippi.

But if you answered C, you're righteous White Trash.

The best way to turn a &%$#up into your advantage is to pretend like you did noble. If you tell your woman you gave the money to Father McGarry, she might be pissed, on account of she thinks Father McGarry is one of them perverts. But she can't be mad too long, on account of women is suckers for doing good deeds.

That means whenever you blow your money, always say something noble, like you bought twenty-five boxes of Girl Scout cookies. Or they got a United Way drive at the plant. Or your girlfriend was short on the rent and you had to front her.

Problem is, pretty soon you gonna run out of noble stuff to say. That means you gotta find an auxiliary loot source.

Enter the boss.

He May Be Evil, but at Least He's Stupid
The Scouting Report:

Raised by yuppies who forced him to play soccer at an early age . . . Wore lots of matching outfits . . . Couldn't get a date for the prom . . . Flunked out of business school . . . Married a beefy woman named Darlene who whines like a opera singer with multiple gunshot wounds . . . Bought a red sports car . . . Failed the real estate exam . . . Got into bossing to take revenge on the world . . .

The good thing about bosses is they ain't very smart. You probably didn't know that boss in Swedish means, "Can somebody show me how to run the copy machine?"

Which means you got the advantage.

Say you laid fifty bucks on St. Louis and seven over the Eagles. A course you lost. What were you thinking, going with the Rams?

Problem is, you already spent most of your noble lies on your woman. So you gotta figure out a new batch of noble stuff to tell your boss so he'll front you your paycheck. Do you:

A. Tell him bad-ass space guys—way meaner than them guys from *Star Trek*—kidnapped you and forced you to bet on the Rams, on account of they don't know no bookies on Earth?

B. Tell him you saw some orphans hanging out in the alley behind your house, so's you kicked their ass on account of you figured it was them who stole your jigsaw last week, but then you found out wrong, so's you had to buy 'em fifty-five bucks worth of Jim Beam to make up for it?

C. Tell him your kid is having an esophagus transplant, and you need fifty-five bucks to cover the co-payment?

D. All of the above.

Seeing as how we're talking about the boss here, all of these lies should work—at least the first couple of times. But after awhile, he'll be getting to suspiciousness. That's why it's best to lie about stuff he don't understand.

Good lies is stuff like, "My daughter's gotta get her pancreas eradicated" or "My wife's getting a skin graft on her uterus."

He won't know what the hell you're talking about, so he'll have to fork over the money, otherwise the guys at the plant'll be laughing at him more than they already do.

But pretty soon them pointy-heads in accounting will figure you got fronted on your paycheck till next July.

They'll cut you off. Which means you gotta get a new batch of lies for Arch-Nemesis No. Three, the bookie.

The Old Rich Uncle from Duluth Trick

This is where the lying gets hard. Bookies is trained professionals. They ain't falling for nothing about pancreases or skin grafting.

Let's look at the situation through his eyes: You bet on the Thrashers and the Rams; he knows you're a moron. You been mumbling about your wife; he knows you're in deep &%$# at home. And the boys from the plant already told him how you ain't got no paychecks coming till July. That means unless you get to some serious lying, he's gonna cash you in.

Which is where the Old Rich Uncle from Duluth Trick comes in.

Tell your bookie you ain't got money this week on account of you had to go see your uncle in the hospital. How it wouldn't be right that you, his favorite nephew— the one he always talked about giving his vending machine company to—didn't visit him on his deathbed.

He'll think you got scratch coming. He'll let you slide.

The next time you can't pay up, tell him you're short cuz you had to go to Duluth again to talk to lawyers. Your uncle's making you executor of his estate, which means your grubs will control the loot.

He'll cut you more slack.

The trick is to string your bookie out like you're catching a carp. First your uncle gets better. Then he goes back at the hospital. Then he got a spleen miscarriage. Then he recovers.

To make it look good, carry a picture of Keith Richards in your wallet. Pretend it's your uncle. Your bookie ain't gonna know the difference. All he knows is the guy looks like he's gonna croak any minute, which means you'll have big scratch to make more stupid bets on the Thrashers and the Rams.

But sooner or later, your bookie will get to figuring there ain't no uncle. By this point, hopefully you're on a winning streak and paid off your debts.

Then again, there ain't a chance in hell of that.

Which leaves you three options:

1. Tell your woman you heard they're hiring at a rendering plant in Arkansas. Get your ass down there right quick.

2. Get beaten to death with a steering wheel lock.

3. Rat your bookie out.

Option One ain't that good. First off, Arkansas is hot and all they ever eat is grits, which is basically Cream of Wheat, only they can't spell that so they call it grits.

Option Two is a little better, seeing as how if you bet on the Rams, you ain't never gonna amount to much anyways. Problem is, by the time you get reincarnated, you're gonna owe a &%$#load of child support.

That leaves Option Three: Rat the guy out. A course, Dr. Verne would never advise nobody to rat—except in special occasions, like saving your own ass.

If you can get a deal for probation, tell the feds all you

know. The bookie goes away for ten years, you clear up your debts, and you can start thinking up new lies to tell your woman.

This here's what financial guys call sound money management.

The White Trash Index

One of the biggest problems for us trash is math. Fact is, you ain't getting on the road to financial security if you don't know what the number thirteen means.

Big Mike understood this. He was our math teacher at the penitentiary, on account of he was in for embezzling from the Kmart lawn and garden department, so's you know he could count.

But he wasn't gonna teach us no calculus, cuz it sounded like it might be Chinese. And since he went to 'Nam, where them Chineses was always shooting at him, he wasn't gonna do 'em no favors by teaching the boys back home no commie math.

So he got to figuring out this special White Trash math on account of it was more useful. You'd just memorize the following list so's you could figure what them big numbers mean. You'd also get clued in on your heritage, seeing as how it was good for winning sucker bets at the bar.

So in honor of Big Mike, who ain't with us no more on account of he got shivved over a pack of GPC menthols, repeat after me. Them funny things that don't look like letters is called numbers. If you don't know what they is, get a guard to explain 'em to you.

Babies needed to discourage your in-laws from thinking you're a lesbian: 6

Legs you'll have left after passing out on train tracks: 0

Average times it takes to pass the driver's license test: 7

Dollars you'll get from a pawnshop for a stolen circular saw: 10

Extramarital affairs for the average White Trash woman: 17

Extramarital affairs for the average White Trash man: 62

Times you've spiked your husband's Old Style with Liquid-Plumr because of that last statistic: 9

Average number of beers consumed at a felony presentencing party: 326

Joints it takes to drive a forklift off a loading dock: 5

Number of beers it takes to bribe the plant urinalysis tester: 100

Proper number of years to wait before repainting your house: 58

Times you've taken a restraining order out against your husband: 11

Average number of people wearing blaze orange hunting jackets at a White Trash wedding: 24

Bags of Beer Nuts you'll get by trading in the antlers of a ten-point buck at a bar in the Upper Peninsula: 39

Average dollar value of the jewelry stolen from the casket at a White Trash funeral: 28

Average number of death threats needed to get your damned HMO to cover your claim for a broken elbow you got in a brawl at Shea Stadium: 4

Number of lies you told to the job service counselor during your weekly meeting: 16

Number of teeth in the average White Trash male over age 27: 8

Shots fired during the average family picnic: 21

Times your uncle Mel's been arrested for indecent exposure: 4

Blows it takes to kill your boss with a claw hammer: 3

Okay, seeing as how all this counting done hurt my head, let's get our ass to the mailbag before our brains blow up and we gotta waste all our duct tape putting our heads back together.

What the &%$# Is a 401(k)?

Dear Dr. Verne:

What the hell is a 401(k)? I've heard the other shop guys talk about it during cig breaks, and I nod my head like I know what they're talking about, but I have no clue. The only thing I know is that I have to decide if I want a little money taken out of my paycheck now so it will pay off later when I'm old.

The whole thing sounds like a great excuse to talk to Becky in the payroll department—she has some bodacious ta-tas—but I want to know what the hell I'm talking about. I don't want to write those newspaper assholes about it because I want my answer in English.

So, Verne, should I sacrifice some cig and Beam money now? Will it really pay off when I retire? Is it true some suit-wearing, bottled-water-drinking pussy from New York will have control of my money?

—Confused in Reno

Dear Confused:

First off, a 401(k) is basically the same as a savings account, except they call it 401(k) cuz it was named by accountants who like giving goofy names to stuff so no one can understand it and you gotta hire their sorry ass.

The good thing about a 401(k) is it gets taken outta your paycheck before you can drink it up. Better yet, your boss, if he ain't a huge cheap-ass like mine, usually kicks in some money, too. This means the boss is actually paying for the Beam you'll be drinking when you retire.

The downside is that you probably ain't never gonna retire, on account of 94 percent of all White Trash die from being mistaken for abandoned kitchen appliances and crushed in garbage compactors before they're sixty-five.

The other downside is some candy-ass from New York is gonna be handling your money, which means he might blow it all investing in wine cooler futures. **At which point you get some guys together from the union and kick his ass, which would be fun, which means it ain't a complete loss.**

Can Chicks Ever Really Respect an Accountant?

Dear Dr. Verne:

Speaking of sorry-ass accountants, I am one. I can't satisfy my wife in bed. Can you tell me how to please a woman?

—*Clueless in San Diego*

Dear Fruity Accountant:

You being an accountant and all, you can't expect your woman to get excited about going to bed with 178 pounds of blubber and gristle. But if you insist on trying, I got some surefire ways to please women, which might even work for accountants.

First off, you gotta set what you call your romantic ambiance. I'd start with some soothing love music, like ZZ Top or Sammy Hagar.

Then I'd make her one of them candlelight dinners. Bring out some nice appetizers, which is what fancy guys call the stuff you eat when you're too hungry to wait for supper. Nothing shows a woman you got class better than deep-fried cheese sticks. But if you don't want to

stink up the house with the deep fryer, just throw some Cheetos in a cereal bowl.

Now most fruity guys %$#& up by going next with a salad. When you make your woman a salad, you're basically saying to her: "I eat the same stuff as rabbits."

I'll clue ya, pal: Women don't get excited about sleeping with rabbits. They're looking for lions, which means you gotta go straight to the main course: potpies.

Nothing says romance better than a turkey potpie. Turkey is a bird, which is kind of like a dove, which is the symbol of love. Make sure you point this out in case she don't get it.

Now she's melting outta your hands.

It's time, my friend, to repair to the bedroom—or the sofa if the bedroom got no TV. This is where a lotta White Trash get stuck. Guys is always asking me, "Yo, Verne, what's the etiquette of watching TV when you're supposed to be satisfying the old lady?"

Me, I judge this by the caliber of the game. Say it's a dainty West Coast game, like the Lakers–Golden State. For that I don't mind turning down the sound. But if it's something good, like Pistons–Cavs, no decent woman should expect to get your full attention. If your woman squawks about stuff like this, you're an asshole for marrying her and you deserve it.

Anyways, at this point you ain't gonna have no problems. The potpies and ZZ Top already got her purring like them babes on the 1-900-NAUGHTY line. All you got to do is sit back, watch Ben Wallace, and let her do the work.

And when she asks about them miraculous sexual powers, don't forget to tell her you learned it all from Dr. Verne.

You Don't Know Nothing About Chicks

Dear Dr. Verne:

I was very disappointed after reading your worthless advice to Clueless in San Diego on how to satisfy a woman in bed. If ZZ Top, Cheetos, and potpies satisfy your White Trash woman, she must be faking it.

To please a woman, a real man needs to learn about a woman's body, pay attention, take a lot of time, and do some of the play/work. You need lessons from a real woman.

—Bay Area Babe

Dear Lady:

First off, I don't appreciate you intruding on my book. This here's some self-help for decent Americans, not people who talk about crap like "empowerment" when they ain't even discussing outboard motors.

Now it sounds like you been going to too

many of them woman studies classes, otherwise you wouldn't be yammering like this. As an expert in this field—seeing as how I seen more backseats in bar parking lots than any man alive—let me clue you in on satisfying the ladies.

Decent White Trash wouldn't be interested in no woman who didn't like ZZ Top and potpies. Right-thinking guys know if their woman is eating fruity &%$# like salads and fifty-eight-grain pasta, they won't got big enough hips to do some quality child-bearing.

Now about faking orgasms: Of course they are. How many ladies you know is gonna have orgasms when they're bedding down with some stinky guy who spent the last ten hours fixing mufflers? That's why White Trash ladies look at guys the same as food: Volume is better than quality.

Take tonight, for your example here. All that's on cable is the Clippers–Phoenix, which is fruity West Coast ball, which means they're going dainty in the paint. Plus, my dart league don't play tonight. Which means I got nothing else to do. Which means me and the little missus is gonna bring the ol' pneumatic drill in for servicing about seventeen times.

Now I ain't claiming all them's gonna be quality operations. But say I hit just .235, which is your basic backup shortstop batting average. That means I'm still knocking down four Big O's a night. You telling me your sensitive ponytail guy can hit with that kind of power?

Now about learning women's bodies: Hell, most White Trash learn this by age four, when they're old enough to steal the old man's *Hustler*.

I hate to say this, lady, but I think you ain't being tolerant of our cultural diversity.

**(You don't wanna be
stuck with no guy
named Chad, do ya?)**

CHAPTER III

ROMANCE
THE WHITE
TRASH WAY

A lot of White Trash men think it's good being a yuppie, seeing as how they get paid way more and don't gotta date women who spit tobacco on the carpet.

Same goes for your White Trash ladies. They figure if they ditch the spandex and quit chewing their gum like some goddamned woodchuck, they could land one of them guys named Chad. The good thing about Chad is he don't smell like roofing tar and got little stockbroker muscles so you can smack 'im around if he gets outta line.

Problem is, yuppie life ain't all it's cracked to be.

Skippy, Brittany, and Why Them Yuppies Ain't Good at Love

Yuppies is like a baby varmint who lost his ma. They're out there all alone in the woods of life, dainty little guys who don't know how to hunt or shoplift. They're defenseless. Which is why they wear them cute sweaters tied around their neck, the international distress signal for "Can someone point me to Old Navy?"

But say you wanna date Chad. And say you gotta bring him home to the family on Thanksgiving for approval. Your uncles is gonna be in the living room watching football and swapping pipefitting stories. They're gonna take one look at Chad, pet him on the head, and make 'im fetch beers all afternoon.

And it ain't gonna look good when your ma sets him a place at the kids' table.

But say you don't believe me yet. Say you're still thinking about dating a yuppie. Let me clue you about your average yuppie date.

Skippy Finds the One

Skippy's talking wine with the waiter, trying to be impressive, like he's got a thin mustache and an ascot or something. The waiter ain't buying, but he ain't letting on either. Each table is worth twenty bucks in tips. Thirty if he kisses ass hard enough. That'll damn near pay a month's worth of cable. And if Skippy's willing to spring for the cable, the waiter's willing to not smack him while Skippy talks outta his ass about wine.

Skippy's looking good tonight. He got the *Beverly Hills 90210* sideburns and so much hairspray it could repel a Tomahawk cruise missile. There ain't no mustard stains on his navy blue blazer. It don't smell like smoke or beer either. You can tell he never wore it to a wedding.

Most guys wouldn't have the balls to wear that tie, all bright yellow and orange and green. But Skippy's going somewheres in this world. The bright colors is his way of saying, "Hey, I got bad taste in ties."

Brittany's his biggest score since Christy Gordter back at Georgetown. Skippy was gonna be a lawyer. Christy was gonna be a trophy wife. She never put out. He still got a complex.

Which is why he flunked the lawyer exam five times. Which is why he's now selling real estate.

These days he's gone to signing his name Emerson "Skippy" Thorwell, EWA, the initials being real estate speak for "I slept through this two-hour seminar and now I got impressive initials after my name." He got a red Chrysler convertible. Cranks the public radio, figuring chicks will think he's deep.

Brittany wears enough makeup that most folks think she oughtta get a hazardous waste permit from the EPA. She went to Yale, majored in English. That's why she's a secretary at a downtown law firm.

They're sitting at the overpriced restaurant, the kind with the cloth napkins and so many goddamned forks you figure the manager's taking kickbacks from a silver-ware salesman.

Skippy's making small talk about how busy it is at the office. How he's gonna close on twenty-three—or was that three?—houses this month. How his clients is always trying to hire him, seeing how professional he is. How he thinks the boss is looking to promote him, let him run his own office. Maybe even get more initials after his name.

Brittany don't make eye contact. Once in a while she nods, throws a smile his way. But mostly she's scoping the room.

She dates three, four, five nights a week. She already slept with all the single guys at the law firm—half the married ones, too. All Brittany wants is to settle down, have some babies, and shop. But now she's twenty-nine. If push come to shove, she'd be willing to skip the first two and just shop.

She ain't impressed by the flowers Skippy got her. Carnations, $9.99 a dozen on sale. She knows the prices of 'em all. And she wasn't impressed by no public radio music either. Her head gets to hurting every time she hears them goddamned violins.

Skippy orders the $29 dinner with the name you can't pronounce. Brittany orders the $43 steak. Why be stupid about it? she figures. He's picking up the tab.

Skippy does the talking over dinner. He tells her how he pumped in 28 points in a pickup basketball game at the Y the other night. How his dad made it rich in the welcome mat business. How the old man wants him to take over the company, seeing as how smart Skippy is.

But he don't want no handouts—except for the red Chrysler and the monthly allowance and the free condo, which don't really count.

Later they go dancing at one of them clubs where the music's so loud you scream at each other like deaf guys. Skippy yells into her ear about how he's thinking on settling down. Just as soon as he gets the big promotion with more money and initials. Probably buy one of them big houses in them golf course subdivisions with the grass that never gets no weeds.

Brittany smiles, one of them smiles that look like they're held up by reinforced steel cable, and goes back to scoping the room. Skippy goes to the can.

A guy named Ted slides up to the bar. He tells Brittany about how he's gonna make partner at the accounting firm he works at. Just as soon as he gets promoted outta the mailroom. She gives him her number.

It's two in the morning. Skippy walks Brittany to her apartment door, then stands there, doing his best impression of a basset who wants out of the rain. She feels obliged to ask him in, seeing as how that steak was forty-three bucks and all.

Skippy makes his move. Brittany don't resist. Might as well, she figures. None of them lawyers call much anymore.

Skippy pumps away on top of her. She thinks of Ted. Could he really go from the mailroom to partner? He must be good at delivering mail. What kind of salaries do partners get? She figures it's gotta be somewhere around the six digits, which's enough to crank some serious firepower into her Marshall Fields card.

She starts shopping in her mind for new blouses, new wallpaper for the kitchen in that gated golf course subdivision that they damn well better get to buying before Skippy snatches it up.

She hears Skippy groan. She starts to squeal, trying to fake an orgasm, but ends up sounding more like one of them squishy bathtub toys. Skippy don't notice. Her squealing is making him feel like Antonio Banderas, or maybe a guy who just got outta prison.

He finally rolls to the side of the bed, trying to catch his breath. Brittany asks him to leave; she's gotta work in the morning. She takes a shower. Skippy lets hisself out.

Brittany meets Ted for lunch the next day. They do the bone dance in the Chili King men's room.

By 10:00 a.m., Skippy's told his ma he's found The One. He'll be bringing her out for Sunday dinner. You're gonna love her, Ma.

He does imitations of Brittany's squeal for the guys at the office. They ain't impressed. It sounds like one of them squishy bathtub toys, they tell him. Skippy don't care. He calls Brittany all afternoon, leaving love poems on her answering machine.

Brittany got sixteen messages when she gets home. She listens to the first few, then erases 'em all. The phone keeps ringing. She lets the machine get it. She's busy, watching Harry Hamlin in a made-for-TV movie.

ROMANCE THE WHITE TRASH WAY   63

She wonders if Harry's married, how much he gets paid, if he ever dates secretaries, or just big stars like Meredith Baxter.

She pulls her knees up to her chest, resting her chin on her sweatpants. She dreams of wallpaper in the gated golf course subdivision where she and Harry's gonna live.

Ronny's White Trash Guide to Courting Proper

In that last section, we learned if you're gonna be a yuppie, chances are you gotta eat food with names you can't pronounce, and your woman's gonna be boning guys named Ted in the Chili King bathroom.

This here section is gonna clue you in on how White Trash is way better at courting, and you get to eat chicken-fried steak.

Ronny's Got a Woman

Ronny's mauling his face with a napkin, trying to get the Thousand Island outta his beard. Eating proper ain't his specialty.

See, Ronny's a big man, going somewheres around six-three, 270. From a distance, he looks like that Abominable Snowman, or maybe just a guy who's got too much liking for pork chops. His is the kinda hands made for pulling engine blocks and laying Sheetrock, not for trying to stuff no bird food in his mouth.

Siss don't seem to mind. It's her first night out in three months.

They're sitting at the Bonanza, wolfing hard on the all-you-can-eat salad bar. Ronny been telling her it's the best in town, on account of it got pickled herring and that chicken-fried steak which looks better than the naked ladies over at B.J.'s Lounge.

Hell, it's kinda romantic too. From where they're sitting, they got a good view of the Radisson, which so happens to be the fanciest hotel in St. Paul. Ronny knows on account of his boss got married there. Had an open bar. He barfed on damn near every inch of that hotel.

Which is why most right-thinking White Trash knows better than to have a open bar.

Ronny, he been married before. Two times. The first one was Linda. She was his high school sweetheart, a dispatcher for Yellow Cab with one of the biggest damn butts you ever seen. Her friends called her Little Canada Butt, on account of she was from Little Canada and had that big butt. Linda, she didn't care. "At least it's paid for," she'd say.

They got married in September. They got separated by October. Divorced before Christmas. Ronny says it's because he came home sick one day and found The Butt in bed with a cabdriver from Pakistan, or maybe Latvia. He couldn't tell which on account of all the blood.

Carla, Ronny's second wife, they was married four years, till she fell asleep in her rig and drove it through a Perkins somewhere in Indiana.

Ronny been thinking about Siss for months. If you was asking him, Siss was the babe to end all babes. But he was ascared to pull the trigger.

Was about six months ago that she dumped her old man. Got herself a job doing invoices at Able's Construction, trying to keep away from the creep. Ronny, he noticed her right away. She had auburn hair that wasn't fake, curled at the ends every day, even when it was raining.

Sure, guys might say she was a bit on the heavy side. But what the hell, Ronny figured. The woman had three kids. If she didn't get to porking out a bit after that, she'd have to be one of them anorexics.

Besides, Siss was the only lady in the office who didn't use the F-word. Always smiled when he dropped by to get his checks. Made a damn fine cup of coffee.

But Ronny never talked to her till the day Phil, her ex, came to the office. Seems Phil was the kind who liked to beat on women, which is why Siss dumped him. But Phil was also on the stupid side. He started yelling about Siss being a bitch right there in the Able office.

Rule number one about cussing your ex-wife: Do it at an insurance agency. Do it at a department store. Do it anywheres they got sissy guys in ties working. But don't go cussing no lady at a construction company.

Ronny was the first to grab Phil. Before you knew, there were six or seven guys on him. They took him outside.

The guys, they still talk about the beating they gave Phil. He looked like the Elephant Man after open-face surgery, all puffy and mangled. These days, he makes sure to pay the child support on time.

Siss appreciated the gesture. Brought Ronny one of them Hostess pies for breakfast the next day to show her thanks. Ronny asked her to dinner. Bonanza. Best eating in town.

Siss makes a third trip to the salad bar. She wolfs down the chicken-fried steak like a guy who just dug 100 yards of postholes. Ronny smiles. Few things is prettier than a woman with a good appetite.

Ronny's telling her how they been Sheetrocking this job over in Highland Park, where a rich man's rehabbing this old railroad mansion. You should see the place, he's telling her. Oak archways. A kitchen practically the size of New Mexico. And a porch that—once they get the rot out and sand down the railings—would be perfect for sipping a little Jim Beam and watching the summertime rain.

Ronny tells her how his goal in life is to buy a place like that. Figures he could pick one up off Seventh Street, in the shade of the old Schmidt plant, for less than 50 grand. Sure, she'll need some work. Maybe take a year or more before it's presentable.

Be nice to settle down in a place like that with a good woman, he tells her, checking to see if she gets the hint. But Siss ain't paying much attention. Damn, that's some good chicken-fried steak.

After dinner, Ronny invites her out to Lou's Viaduct Inn. It's a classy place, he tells her. Got computer darts and 50-cent pool and drinks for a buck-fifty. Damn if that bartender Jerry don't make the best fuzzy navel in town. The ladies sure go for that.

But Siss says she gotta go. Things is still tight at home. Got to get rid of the babysitter before the bill gets too high. Besides, she's probably got her clothes half off with her boyfriend right now.

Ronny says he understands, tries to smile, but he knows he's getting the high hat. He wonders what he did wrong. Was it the cole slaw that kept getting in his beard? The time he accidentally cut the cheese while they was waiting at the biscuit tray?

He knows the guys at the bar'll ride him hard if he comes back alone. Hell, it's only eight o'clock. They drive home without talking.

At the door, Ronny tells her how much he enjoyed his-self. How it was a pleasure to have the company of such a fine lady. He asks if she wouldn't mind him paying the babysitter, seeing as how times was tight.

Siss pecks him on the cheek. Asks if he wouldn't mind coming in. Her sister borrowed her a couple of Chuck Norris videos to watch. Did Ronny like Chuck Norris?

Ronny follows her in, even though he thinks Chuck Norris is a fruity. The guy's always wearing turtlenecks, for chrissakes. Now he's got a TV show about Texas Rangers. Pussy. If he was a real cop, he'd be working in a place that got better crime, like Detroit or Pittsburgh, not busting some cattle rustlers who's dressed up like tour guides from South Dakota.

But Ronny ain't letting on. "Yeah, I love that guy," he tells her.

The kids is all in their pajamas, running around the living room like drunk Teamsters at the end of a strike. The babysitter's on the phone, fighting with her boyfriend, who just so happens to be her cousin too.

It's a nice-looking place, Ronny thinks to hisself. Decent panel job, whoever did it. Good couch too. Still got the plastic on so it don't get no baby drool. Siss got her wedding pictures on the wall, only Phil's been crossed out with a marker.

Siss sends the babysitter home, puts the two littlest to bed. Her oldest girl sits between 'em on the couch as Chuck pretends he's a Chicago cop on TV. He's wearing that goddamned turtleneck again. Chuck would get his ass kicked if he ever showed up at Lou's, Ronny thinks to hisself.

Siss' oldest is a good kid. She got big ears and her teeth kinda look like the mangled grill of an old Dodge, but she's cute in her own way. Ronny wouldn't mind calling her his own, on account of he never had none for hisself. The Butt was too busy boning cabdrivers from Pakistan or Latvia to get to reproducing. Carla always said she'd have some, but that ended when she left her Mack in the no smoking section of that Indiana Perkins.

One of the little ones is crying in the bedroom. Siss goes to lay with him, says she'll be right back. Hour later, she still ain't there. Ronny puts in another Chuck and lets the oldest lay on his lap.

The next morning, Siss finds him sleeping on the couch. The TV's still running, and Ronny's snoring louder than the grinder at the packing plant she used to work at. Her oldest is snuggled under one of his arms.

She makes him bacon and eggs. He shovels her driveway and rehangs her gutters on account of the roof is rotting.

Siss' sister comes over late in the morning. Siss blabs to her like a schoolgirl about the nice man she found. How much her kids like him. How he made Phil look like the Elephant Man. How he's outside right now fixing the gutters, which she'd been on Phil about for more than a year. That prick.

There's still decent men out there, Siss says. You just gotta look.

Ronny comes in to let Siss know the gutters is done. He sees her blabbing, figures it's time to go. Got some work to do, he says.

But Ronny don't feel like working. It's Sunday afternoon. The Vikings is on. He heads over to Lou's, where the guys'll be.

Ronny orders up a Schmidt. The guys want to know how it went. Did he get any? Was her boobs really as big as they looked?

Ronny tells 'em to shut up. Tells 'em that gentlemens don't talk about a lady like that, and if you creeps was gentlemens you'd know that. But he can't be pissed at 'em. He can't be pissed at the Vikings either, who's down by ten to Jacksonville.

He sits at the bar, staring at the big screen. All he can think about is a place off Seventh Street, Siss' kids playing in the house, and him sitting on the porch, sipping on some Jim Beam and watching that summertime rain.

The Token Section About Deep and Cultural Stuff

"Verne, you gone fruity?"

That's probably what you're thinking right now on account of I got this part about deep and cultural stuff. But here's the thing:

In the last section, we done learned from Ronny how to get to sparking proper. Problem is, even if you got a top-shelf woman like Siss, sooner or later watching Chuck Norris and rehanging the gutters ain't gonna get you to your third round of wedded bliss.

See, women is prone to thinking about them fineries on occasion. Which means that one day she's gonna up and announce that she wants you to take her someplace classy. And that means the two most dreaded words in the White Trash language is gonna come outta her lips: "art museum."

Now don't call no doctor. There ain't no cure for this disease. It's called epilepsy, which is medical talk for "Christ, I got a bad idea."

It's just like the flu, but instead of giving you an excuse to sleep on the porch all day, it makes you suddenly go weird and wanna do dumb-assed things, like go to the art museum.

Now them epilepsies usually show up about Sunday afternoon, after you spent all weekend laying on the couch watching the Orioles–Toronto series. Your woman's gonna get the notion to haul your ass outta the house, so's you can have some deep quality time together.

Of course you're gonna protest. "Sit your ass down," you say in your most lovey voice. "Ain't no better art than watching Miguel Tejada play the deep short on Astroturf."

Which, of course, means she's gonna slap you harder than a truckstop waitress.

Which means you best get your ass moving, unless you wanna be eating White Castle for the next month.

Now you gotta spend the afternoon surrounded by pointy-heads with berets, who's gonna stare like you're some kind of moron for wearing your Titans Zubaz and the Loren's Mobile Home Retirement Community T-shirt your ma sent up from Orlando.

But don't go aworrying. Faking like you're clued in on deep stuff is easier than hijacking a truckload of laundry softener. Just listen to your ol' pal Verne.

How to Be Held in Rapture

The first thing you notice at museums is that everybody wears black. It's like they're in mourning cuz their ma's all died at once.

This is the official uniform of Authentic Deep People.

Now Deep People ain't good for much. They can't fire-bomb a scab's house or clean a walleye. But they're awful good at standing around museums staring at stuff and not saying a word, as if they drank a fifth of Jack and is watching *Naughty Car Wash Babes III*.

But they ain't drunk. They're just held in rapture.

I don't exactly know what rapture is, but it's important to being deep. The trick is to stare at a painting or sculpture for a long time, pretending it's so meaningful it cut off your tongue. Then, after about a half-hour, say something about its "gripping isolation" or its "transcendent insight into the systematic betrayal of faith," just so folks don't think you're a mute.

It don't matter that no one will know what the hell you're talking about. That's the point of being deep.

Faking Like You Know French

If there was truth in advertising, most paintings would be titled, "Globs of Paint Thrown on Canvas and Hocked at a Gallery Because I Had to Pay the Rent."

Problem is, Deep People figure this stuff got metaphors and symbolism in it. Which brings us to lesson number one: Always pretend art has meaning, even if it looks like it was knocked out by a two-year-old who got a hold of some latex while her ma was on the phone.

Say you're at a museum with the old lady, and you're staring at an eighty-foot canvas with one red dot in the middle. Strike a deep and thoughtful pose, hand on chin, like you're captivated by its power. Then, after a long silence, say something French.

Of course, you don't know no French. Which is why you gotta use the names of hockey players: "I find a disturbing sense of *gaetan duschene* in her work."

The Beret People will be intimidated by your deepiocity. They won't notice that the painting reminds you of a former winger for the Minnesota North Stars.

The Performance Art Scam

Before the 1960s, this was called Stuff People Do Before Becoming a Ward of the State Mental Hospital. Then someone figured out that Deep People would pay top dollar to see loonies.

So a bum, tired of sleeping on heating grates, laid down on the floor of the Chicago Museum of Art, stuffed himself in a giant Ziploc bag, and called his work "This Is Just as Good a Place as Any to Sleep."

Performance art was born.

The bum became the toast of the Wine and Brie Circuit. One problem: He suffocated to death.

So some other bums cashed in when they left his body in the museum to rot, calling their project "Works in Decomposing Carcass."

They are now tenured professors at Berkeley and get to sleep in their offices.

Sculpture's Red Green Period

There was a day when you could slap up an eight-footer of some naked Greek guy and everyone was happy. Problem was, everybody could understand it, which means no one could feel superior, which means it wasn't very good art.

In order to become deeper, sculptors started welding rusty Viking grills and old lawn furniture together, calling it "Interdisciplinary Works in Stuff Welded Together That the Artist Couldn't Unload at His Garage Sale." They claimed it was a metaphor for the decline of Western Civilization.

The Red Green Period was born.

It ain't easy to fake your way through this stuff. But a few handy lines will help you pawn yourself off as one of them aficionados of sculpture.

Say you're trying to hit on the babe from the plumbing fixtures aisle at Home Depot. She's going to night school at the community college, taking up legal secretarying. You figure she's gotta be deep.

So you take her to the new exhibit of the noted New York sculptor to see his greatest work: a propane tank painted with white enamel. Okay, so it's just a propane tank, for chrissakes. But being deep and all, you fake like you're held speechless.

After the standard period of silence, you say something like, "Its lines speak to a piercing violation of the human psyche."

Then, you add, "I've always admired his work with utility industry hardware."

If the Beret People nearby nod their approval, say something critical. (Lesson number two: You can't be deep if you ain't always bitching about something.) Compare his work to another hockey player.

"Of course," you sniff, "his work is not equal to Lucien LaFreniere's, who was the master of the propane genre."

LaFreniere had a cup of coffee with the Islanders in the mid-'80s. Nobody'll know what the hell you're talking about. Which means you're deeper than them.

"Yes," they will agree as they slink away, intimidated by your insight. "LaFreniere was the forerunner of the modern propanists."

Your babe will think you're cultural. She'll want you to spend the night at her place.

If There's No Unshaven Detectives, It Must Be Deep

Sometimes art museums got movies. But you're supposed to call 'em films.

Film means it was directed by some guy with a thin mustache from Europe who don't read box scores.

Movie means it was directed by some guy who's originally from Nebraska, but dyed his hair blonde, moved to Hollywood, and started saying stuff like, "Love ya, babe. *Ciao.*"

If it got no action and has subtitles and the camera stays glued to some lady for fifteen minutes while she stares out the window and looks like her best hunting dog died, it's a film.

But if it's got unshaven detectives who break department rules to work with big-boobed babes to hunt down international terrorists with crewcuts named Hans, it's a movie.

Say you're a woman who just got a job in the claims department at Mephistopheles Insurance. And say you got a hankering for the boss. He ain't that good looking, but he's a boss, which means he probably got ice cream and a good liquor cabinet back at his place.

So you pull out the skimpy wardrobe you got from your sister, who didn't need it no more after she quit the strip joint when she had her sixth kid.

It works. He asks you for a date before lunchtime.

But instead of taking you to a bar, like decent trash, he

takes you to some goddamned film festival about the great directors of Greenland. So you gotta fake like you're deep. Otherwise, you ain't scoring none of that liquor and ice cream.

The key to faking a film knowledge is citing the great masters.

So say you just done spent four hours on some double-feature with subtitles. You don't even know what language they was talking. As you stroll from the theater, say something like, "Ah, touches of Fellini."

Your boss won't call your bluff. He's an insurance guy, for chrissakes. He thinks Greenland's an amusement park in Vermont.

"However," you add, "the cinematic minimalism was preponderantly influenced by Bergman, wouldn't you agree?"

This is a lock to work, since everybody knows the masters is supposed to be deep, but nobody's ever seen their movies.

Your boss will nod his head in approval. He will realize you're deeper than him. He will change the subject to his theories on term life policies.

And the next time you go out, he'll take you to a *Die Hard* sequel.

I'm thinking it was Shakespeare who done said, "Love is a many-splendored thing."

You know what he's talking about? Me neither. But it proves a valuable point.

See, Shakespeare was from the olden days when they pranced around in wigs and tights. And since wigs and tights guys knows stuff about flowers and interior decorating, they're also supposed to know about love. And seeing as how some candy-ass like Shakespeare don't even know what he's talking about, that just shows how complicated proper sparking really is.

So let's get to the mailbag, cuz I know you got questions.

My Girlfriends Say I Gotta Set Boundaries with Earl

Dear Dr. Verne:

I got me my mobile home from my ex in the divorce decree. While I been divorced from Earl for five months, I been letting him sleep over. I'm between men right now, and while he's not what I call a one-woman man, we do got us a history and two kids together.

Anyhow, now that our Saturday nights have become regular and all, he feels the trailer is his again. He's been leaving his beater truck in the yard. It's without a engine and you got to ride it Indian style, seeing how's there ain't no floorboard.

Well, Verne, my girlfriends say I gotta set boundaries. What the hell does that mean?

I mean, he ain't asked me to tattoo his name on my hindquarters, like he asked me when we was hitched. I just feel maybe I should draw the line somewheres, but least I get some lovin' and Earl leaves his Wild Turkey bottles and Old Mil cans for me to cash in so I can get the wee ones beans and Tang.

             —*Cherri, Burlington, Vermont*

Dear Cherri:

Boundaries is one of them things the feminisms thought up. Here's the best way to explain it:

Think of yourself as a motel. Seeing as how you're single and on the prowl again, you want to make sure that "vacancy" sign is always lit up, just in case some guy with a good back injury settlement wanders by and figures he might stop in for a spell.

But seeing as how Earl's hanging around, he's like a big "no vacancy" sign. So the back injury guy is gonna figure your motel got occupied, and he's gonna stop at the neighbor lady's instead, on account of she's got nicer trucks parked on her yard.

Which means as long as Earl's there, your motel's gonna be empty. Which means you ain't gonna show no weary traveler the full bouquet of your female-like hospitalities, if you get what I'm saying.

Which is a long way of saying them feminisms want you to kick Earl's ass out.

Now I'm hearing you about it being good to

have a man around and all. Even if he's a stiff, he can still cut the grass and haul old car batteries to the compost pile. Plus it's always good having someone to bitch at when you're crabby or out of liquor.

Problem is, you don't wanna get too cozy.

Say you meet one of them guys who does oil changes at Tires Plus. The guy probably makes top dollar, like $7.50 an hour, plus bennies. And say you take him home some night. It ain't gonna be good for starting no healthy relationship if Earl's passed out naked on the kitchen floor.

If I was you, I'd get me some of them boundaries. Start by telling Earl he gotta sleep in the truck just in case you bring the Tires Plus guy home. Let him know he can only sleep in the house when you're horny and there ain't no other decent men around.

Second off, don't let him use the remote. Nothing makes a man feel more unwanted than not getting to touch the channel surfer.

Last but not least, tattoo somebody else's name on your hindquarters, like Mel or Tires Plus. It don't matter who it is. Earl will be able to tell by your butt that he's permanently outta the picture, and that he should go back to Wanda, the broad he dumped you for when you got divorced in the first place.

If none of this works, shoot him. Men get to understanding real good when they got some buckshot in 'em.

Our Bud Is Getting Held Hostage in the Suburbs

Yo Verne, You Dawg:

We need help. One of our buds got drug to the suburbs by his ol' lady. Better than his ol' double-wide, she said.

We've been worried about him, but he's trying to make it right by not tying his sweaters around his neck or trading in his F-150 extended cab for a wuss Isuzu Trooper.

He keeps making noises 'bout putting a dirty mattress, a couple of buckets of the Colonel's extra greasy, and nine or ten twelvers of Busch in the back for partying with the girls from the strip joint. But when push comes to shove, he keeps drinking Zima and talking about racquetball.

What can we do to help 'im get back on the Beam and not get us in jail or shot by his woman?

—Bob & Ray, Windsor, Ontario

Dear Fellas:

Sounds to me like your bud got converted over to the dark side. He's in the hands of the devil. This calls for one of them exorcisms. You're gonna need a priest and plenty of liquor.

Now the key to exorcisms is using his devil

ideas against him. See, them yuppies is always trading in their used girlfriends. They get to sparking with a babe, but pretty soon she's pounded them quiches like a longshoreman who just got back from sea. Next thing you know, their woman's the size of a decent strong safety.

Now good trash knows there ain't nothing wrong with a woman who got a little beef on her, specially if you's planning on stealing some scrap iron, which is damn heavy hauling by yourself. Besides, if God wanted women to be perfect, he woulda made 'em into bass boats instead.

But them yuppies don't like ladies who got a little worn tread, on account of it don't impress nobody at the company golf outing.

Since your buddy is probably already brainwashed in them fruity suburb ways, bribe the priest with some liquor so he'll tell your bud that his woman is looking a might craggy these days. Seeing as how he's a priest, he ain't gonna be partial to no babe over the age of fourteen anyways.

Your bud will dump his yuppie woman like a bad slice of ham. And since she got all the loot, he'll be sleeping on your couch in no time.

Then you can hook him to a decent lady, the kind who got big hair and puts on her makeup with a power painter. Once he gets in them ever-loving arms of some genuine trash, consider the guy cured.

Locusts, Famine, and Forty Years of Flatulence

Dear Dr. Verne:

Me and my buddy, Galen, we owns a drywalling business. A couple weeks ago we was hanging and mudding some rock on a remodel job in one of them strip malls in the suburbs.

In the strip mall was one of them wussy bars. Galen (he's a real bird dog) kept noticing these good-looking yuppie chicks going into this wussy bar.

Now those yuppie chicks don't do nothing for me, but Galen says that all babes, even those yuppie babes, deserve to have a real man once in a while.

So one night after work Galen and I wandered down to the wussy bar only because I wanted to do what was right. Well, one of them yuppie babes got kinda friendly with me. We ended up back at her place and she got real friendly with me, if you know what I mean.

The next morning I woke up and smelled the worst smell I ever sniffed. I asked the yuppie babe what the hell was the smell. She said, "I just have a little flatulence."

Verne, I was real scared. I don't know what flatulence is.

Now Galen, he's got a real smart son, Galen Jr.,

by either his second or third wife. Hell, Galen Jr. is so smart he almost got into the sheet metal apprentice program.

Anyways, Galen Jr. thinks that the flatulence may be one of them sexually transmitted diseases. Verne, should I be soaking something in kerosene?
—Stan the Drywall Man, Providence

Dear Stan:
I'm thinking this flatulence is one of them Bible things. Say too many people get to stealing and drinking and coveting thy neighbor's woman, which makes Moses pissed. So he orders up one of them forty years of flatulence, which means floods and locusts and famine. That way people know not to &%$# with Moses.

I asked the barmaid at Johnny's Tavern if this was right. She said yeah. But what she don't got figured is why that yuppie babe was talking about locusts when her apartment got to stinking.

Me, I figure she was just trying to impress you with big words, seeing as how you got your own business and you'd probably take her to the Indian casino every night if you was married.

But the barmaid, she figures that yuppie babe was worried about Moses putting forty years of flatulence on her for sinning. If she was decent and God-fearing, He woulda born her with spandex and nine kids already. But since she's taken to them Godless yuppie ways, she knows Moses'll be more ornery than a foreman who just got his child support jacked.

Next time you sees that yuppie babe, give her a five-gallon bucket of Ortho. She's gonna need it for when them locusts show up.

(Or, How to Get Lots
of Weddings So
People Don't Think
You Might Be a
Homo)

CHAPTER IV
MARRIAGE

When God created the world, He started out with woman, seeing as how she had more complex architecture and plumbing. Besides, He was dying for conversation cuz He hadn't invented TV yet.

Anyways, it took Him damn near all week—three days working on the brain alone.

Then, late on the Sixth Day, the hardware stores was closed. Knowing that He wouldn't get overtime for working Sunday, God just slapped together man with the leftover scraps and headed for the bar.

Which is why men ain't too smart. He figured if He just made 'em strong enough to carry in the groceries, there might be a use for 'em.

Ten Tips for Women Who's Ascared of Getting Stuck with a Loser

This here's what you call your ten-point checklist for finding yourself some husbands. It's to help you decide the difference between a worthless man—one who ain't great, but good enough to have babies with—and a low-down, nasty, lying, cheating man, who's only good for affairs.

Now when it comes to men, the selection ain't good. But think of it like rummaging through the clothes bins at Goodwill. At least you got volume on your side.

1. Is he a pervert?

All men is perverts. But there's a big difference between regular perverts and gentlemen perverts. Regular perverts take you to Hooters on your first date and spend the night telling stories about the biggest jugs they ever seen. Which ain't classy, especially if they only got enough money for chicken wings.

Gentlemen perverts is at least self-respecting enough to buy you a decent meal and some plastic jewelry before trying to get you in the sack.

If your old man A.) named his reproductive unit after a World War II cargo plane; B.) still subscribes to *National Geographic* for the naked Amazon babes; or C.) is a lawyer, chances are he's a pervert. Don't let him near your kids.

2. Does he live with his ma?

If he still lives with his ma, he's used to getting picked up after, which means you won't have time for affairs with the guys from the Paint & Sealant Department.

The good part is he's a mama's boy who'll be easy to smack around when he squawks about your making hot dogs for supper sixteen days in a row. The bad part is he'll be too sissified to teach your kids the valuable lessons of life, like how to sweet-talk the game warden when you're four muskies over limit.

It's best to get a guy who's been on his own for a few years. That way, if you clean every Christmas and don't ash on the carpet, he'll think you're Martha Stewart.

3. Does he work at a convenience store?

Convenience stores is bad for two reasons. First off, he'll only make six bucks an hour, which means a day's work only buys a thirty-pack of diapers and a twelver of Grain Belt.

Second off, convenience store clerks is always getting shot. What happens if you got a big night at the Legion Hall planned, the old man gets shot, and he ain't home to babysit on time?

4. Can he fake a decent back injury?

A lot of women is attracted to stupid guys cuz they'll believe it when you tell 'em stuff like, "If you don't run to the store and get me some cigs, you can catch AIDS." But he can't be too stupid.

Say your old man's faking a back injury to score workers' comp. But say his buddy, who's a contractor, offers him a side job busting a concrete driveway, which just happens to be at the house of his caseworker, Reginald Grabowski.

The first clue might have been the name "Reginald Grabowski" stenciled on the mailbox.

But your old man, figuring there's gotta be dozens of Reginald Grabowskis in Powell Butte, Oregon, keeps slugging away with the maul. Next thing you know, he loses the workers' comp.

Yet he ain't smart enough to do the logical thing: Smash his foot with the maul, so he can get another workers' comp scam going.

That's why you don't wanna make no more than three babies with stupid guys. When you're old, your kids won't know how to scam either. They'll be nobody around to buy you vodka and Lotto tickets.

5. Is he a fat pig?
This can be good or bad, depending on how you look at it. Most women don't like being married to a fat pig cuz it's like sleeping with a walrus. If you was attracted to walruses, you'd probably marry a real one, on account of zoo animals don't pay no rent and people throw food at you.

The good part is, if your old man gets fat enough, you can use him for insulation when the heat gets shut off.

6. Is he dainty?

Does your old man spend more time talking about his hair dryer than his power tools? Does he put mousse in his caulking gun? Does he have problems saying who's the points leader in the Winston Cup standings?

If so, he's probably a lawyer, which means he's good at bilking old ladies' trust funds, but he'd end up being a love toy for the Aryan Nation if he went to prison. The ladies at the beauty parlor won't respect no woman who's sharing her man with a 320-pound guy named Otis, so you'll have to start cutting your hair with a hedge trimmer.

7. Does he got manners?

You can tell a real gentleman cuz he'll always say something nice about your butt, no matter how big it is.

Say he's laying on the couch watching baseball. "Woman," he says, "could you score me another brewski?" As you leave the room he adds, "Your butt's so cute I should list it on the renter's insurance as precious jewelry."

That's class.

But what if he only says, "Woman, grab me another brewski." Then, as you leave the room, all he does is cuss out Troy Percival for giving up a two-out single. This here's an example of no class, which means you should probably set him up with your sister. Then you can gossip about the moron she married at family get-togethers.

8. Does he flirt with other women?

This could be a sign that he's hound dogging truckstop waitresses when he's supposed to be at the strip joint with his buddies. Then again, a lotta ladies don't mind their men having affairs cuz they'll do less pawing on them. If it keeps the creep outta the house, all the better. Just make sure his ass is around when it's time to shovel the sidewalk.

9. Does he eat sissy?

Say your old man wants to propose. He's offering to take you to dinner, someplace classy. Naturally, you pick KFC. But all the way there he's talking about saturated fat and cholesterol.

Dump him.

If he don't like KFC, chances are he jogs and has a matching tennis outfit he hides at his ma's house. If you marry him, he'll be too dainty to defend your honor when your uncle paws your butt during the dollar dance at the wedding.

10. Does he still brag about his glory days?

Nothing worse than having an old man who thinks he's an athlete. Whenever he gets drunk, he'll be giving you the frame-by-frame account of how he won the rec league bowling title when he was fourteen.

Worse yet, you'll have to haul your ass to softball games all summer, making excuses to the other wives about why your husband couldn't snare a grounder if it was a naked lady with a twelve-pack.

Ten Tips for Keeping Guys Outta Divorce Court (at Least Till Next Month)

Okay, fellas, this ain't TV. Only morons figure they're gonna score a total babe who can fry up a bass and hold a decent conversation about the New Orleans secondary.

The way I figure it, shopping for women is like shopping for trucks. Sure, you want the extended cab with the brush guard, snow plow, and the heavy-duty suspension. But if you score half that, you're doing pretty good.

That's why I got this ten-point checklist. If your woman passes five or more, it's safe to pull the trigger.

Now this don't guarantee nothing. But according to the rules of White Trash Etiquette, you got at least eleven divorces before people start looking at you weird.

1. Make sure she ain't a pig

You don't want no wife who cleans like a drunk maid from one of them rent-by-the-hour motels. That's why you gotta do research. Ask yourself these questions: Does she draw Easter decorations in the grease on the kitchen wall? Does she leave cig butts in the shower drain? Is the crumbs on her carpet thick enough to clean with one of them leaf blowers?

If you're answering yes, you're gonna need a night job to pay for the maid.

2. Make sure she don't got a sister who's way better looking

Say you knock up your woman. Then, on your wedding night, you finally meet her sister from Kansas, who's way better looking than the one you're marrying. Next thing you know you'll be trying to score with her in the garage at family gatherings. Romance ain't real pleasurable with a Lawn Boy stuck in your back.

What's more, your woman's brothers'll get wind of it and beat you till you talk like a figure skater.

Ask to see the family pictures before you get to knocking her up.

3. Can she cook a decent steak?

Nothing worse than working hard all month to collect the unemployment check, then having your woman make a steak that looks like it got cooked by an arc welder.

It ain't a bad idea to road test her on the cooking before you get to the wedding bells. Have her cook a steak after she just pounded a quart of Beam, or after you just got home with lipstick on your pants zipper and called her Lucy by mistake.

If she can still nail the steak under these normal conditions, you got yourself a keeper.

4. Can you whup her ex?

The first time your woman takes her ex to court for being behind on the child support, he's gonna show up at your place. What you gotta know is, can you kick his ass? And if you can't, is it worth shooting him, seeing as how dead guys don't usually pay support and you'll probably have to get a job?

5. Make sure she ain't no temperance woman

Say you and your buddies drop by the bar after work. And say one of 'em is celebrating because his daughter got outta prison. He wants to buy a round of shots. But you gotta pass, on account of your woman will squawk if you come home hammered for dinner.

Pretty soon all your buddies is gonna look at you like you got naked pictures of Barbara Bush hanging in your garage.

Never marry a woman who got less than two drunk-driving arrests. If she's a lush herself, she may clean the liquor cupboard out, but at least you won't have to apologize when you park the truck in the living room.

6. Watch out for them woman's equalities

It's okay if ladies want equal pay. Then they can buy rounds too. But there's two things a guy's gotta have total control over: the channel surfer and the power tools.

If she don't understand this, she's probably from California. Unload her before you go fruity and start drinking wine that don't come in a box.

7. Is her hips sturdy enough for baby making?

The last thing you want is some skinny lady who whines like a college boy during labor. Chances are she's gonna cut you off at two kids. Which means the guys down at the plant'll be calling you a wuss cuz you don't have enough little shavers for a pit crew.

Me, I'd take her to the doc and get her hips measured. If they ain't baby-making caliber, get yourself one of them prenuptial agreements that says if she don't give you at least five babies, you can trade her in for a real wife.

8. Will she pork out on you?

A lot of women start out skinny, have five or eight kids, then get to looking like a Coast Guard flotation device. If she thinks a two-pound bag of Doritos is a before-supper appetizer, you're looking at some serious oatmeal butt down the road.

The good part is she'll be too fat to get a job as a stripper or have affairs with your cousins. The bad part is that making love will be like wrestling a giant Polish sausage.

9. Does she got a union job?

Union jobs is better than winning the lottery, on account of you can't drink it all up in one night. If she's good at earning and saving, you can stay home and play Mr. Mom.

This ain't as wussified as it sounds. Just feed the kids donuts and let 'em play in the street. Meanwhile, you can spend your days at the hardware store or watching reruns of monster truck rallies on satellite.

10. Will she rat you out?

Last thing you want is a woman who ain't honest. If you get caught in bed with your aunt, she might get pissed and tell the cops about all them highway signs you stole for scrap aluminum.

So how do you tell if she's honest? Ask if she'd rather sleep with you or Billy Ray Cyrus. If she says you, dump her before she rats you out on that feed mill burglary you did last week.

Okay, so I know you got worries about pulling off your wedding days. Say you got kin coming in from one of them cultural, cosmopolitan cities, like Mobile, Alabama, so you wanna show some class. Or say you's getting married someplace in Texas, and you know the guests is gonna have more guns than a Hezbollah Fourth of July picnic.

If you put on a bad show, your uncles is gonna start shooting at the church ceiling just to liven things up. That's when the ATF shows up. A firefight breaks out.

You's gonna have a lotta leftover bologna if all your guests get shot and lose their appetite.

So let's fetch that mailbag and get down to the serious wedding planning. But don't go a worrying. You're trash. If you %&$@ up this wedding, there's gonna be plenty more where that came from.

Is Eloping Bad Financial Management?

Dear Dr. Verne:

I'm engaged to Rocco, but I haven't told my daddy yet. He thinks Rocco's a lazy ass and says if he ever catches me and him together, he'll cut out his throat with a chainsaw.

I tell him Rocco just got his GED and his old man's getting him on at the sanitation department, but daddy won't listen. I want to elope, but Rocco says that's bad financial management, on account of we'll miss out on all them presents. What should I do?

—Shonda in Trenton

Dear Shonda:

This Rocco's a keeper. He's got smarts enough to realize no matter how big of a scumbag he is, the rules of weddings say your folks still gotta give you presents. And seeing how Rocco's old man got a decent union job, you guys'll probably be into the serious presents, like power augers and season tickets to the Eagles.

Plus, it don't really matter if your old man slices up Rocco anyways. That just means instead of taking him to the Eagles game, you could take that A&P clerk you been sleeping with. He's probably got more money to buy you some beers and brats anyways.

A Question of Class: Charcoal Gray or Powder Blue?

Dear Dr. Verne:

I'm marrying a handsome young man from Eugene. I know you won't approve, seeing as how he's from a dainty college town, but I love him just the same.

Anyways, I been fighting with his mom about the wedding. She wants the groomsmen to wear charcoal gray. But I don't want my man wearing anything you burn in a power plant or cook hamburgers with.

I figure he should wear a powder blue tux. It looks way prettier, and will hide the barf stains if he gets too drunk.

But since she's paying for the wedding, she wants it her way. Bitch. I don't think that's right.

—*Tammy in Seattle*

Dear Tammy:

Everyone knows powder blue is superior. If he was to dress up in some charcoal, chances are he'd get eaten by a pack of dogs, on account of they know that smell means good eating. But that's what you get for consorting with a lesser class of people.

What you gotta do is express your feelings. Let your mother-in-law know this is your wedding, and that she should shut her mouth or you're gonna do it with a roofing stapler. If that don't work, grab her by the hair when no one's looking, and dunk her head in the toilet till she stops breathing.

This is what feminisms call being assertive. If she ain't breathing, that means she can't do no talking. And that means you don't have to marry no guy who's dressed up like a hamburger.

What's the Seating Arrangements for Inbred Weddings?

Dear Dr. Verne:

I'm gonna marry my cousin Billy in August. Problem is, we don't know which side of the aisle to seat the guests, seeing how both of us is related.

—Mary in Fort Kent, Maine

Dear Mary:

Basic science says that none of your relatives is gonna have a clue, seeing as how they're inbreds. I'd worry more about getting 'em to use the chairs instead of laying on the floor. Arm your ushers with some cattle prods just to be on the safe side.

How's a Guy Supposed to Stop His Relatives from Stealing the Silverware?

Dear Dr. Verne:

I got it made. I'm getting married to Sandy Bluderhousen. Her face ain't that good, but she's got a nice body and her old man runs the biggest construction company in Wyoming.

Here's my problem: Sandy's old man is springing for a reception at the Super 8. But I'm worried my relatives is gonna steal the silverware. I don't want Sandy's old man pissed at me, otherwise he won't give me one of them no-show jobs.

—Louie in Casper

Dear Louie:
One of the hottest things in weddings this year is metal detectors. That not only keeps your relatives from stealing the silverware, it also keeps 'em from bringing guns, knives, and bats to the reception, which makes for fairer fights.

The last thing you need is one of your brothers getting liquored up and stabbing your father-in-law when he turns him down for a job. According to wedding experts, whacking in-laws ain't a healthy way to start a marriage. With metal detectors, you not only save on having to reimburse the hotel for all the stuff that gets stoled, but all the knife fights will be in the lobby, where they ain't your problem.

Who's My Daddy?

Dear Dr. Verne:

I'm getting married, but my ma don't know exactly who my daddy is. The way she figures it, it could be one of about twenty guys who used to hang out at Myron's Tavern in Rockford in 1987. Which one should I ask to give me away?

—Monica in Kankakee, Illinois

Dear Monica:
I'd use what you call your deductive reasoning here. You figure half of 'em gotta be dead or in prison, which knocks it down to ten.

Then I'd knock out the two ugliest ones, on account if they're your father, you don't wanna know.

Then I'd kick out the four that don't got no money, seeing how what's the use of getting a dad if he ain't gonna give you nothing for your troubles?

Now you're down to four. Here's where the picking gets easy.

I'd tell 'em there's an open bar and invite 'em all. The one who's smart enough to drive all the way from Rockford gotta be your dad, on account of the other three's too stupid to get down your ma's pants if they ain't smart enough to go where the free liquor is at.

How to Hide the Fact That You're Knocked Up

Dear Dr. Verne:

I be getting married in February, but I'm already in the motherly way, if you know what I mean. What wedding gown would you recommend for hiding pregnancies?

—Lucy in Black River Falls, Wisconsin

Dear Lucy:

Seems you got two choices here. The first is to wear a normal wedding dress, on account of most people will just think you got a beer belly. That'll tell your husband's kin you're decent, down-home people, and you like a beer and a steak just as much as the next guy.

But if you wanna play this sneaky—which I don't know why you would, cuz most White Trash women got a whole litter before they're married—I'd think about going casual. Wear something with class, like your Arctic Cat jacket or a Packers jersey. This sends a message to the audience that you got a pioneering sense of fashion, and that you ain't some moron who's gonna blow sixteen bucks on a fancy wedding dress when it could pay for the whole first night of your honeymoon at Warren's Motor Lodge.

How Am I Gonna Get Rid of All Them Blenders?

Dear Dr. Verne:

I'm worried about getting hitched. First off, how's a guy supposed to be married when there's so many barmaids I ain't nailed yet?

Second off, I figure I'm gonna end up with seventeen blenders and no place to hock 'em. What you gotta say about that?

—Harry, underneath the 9th Street Bridge

Dear Harry:

Don't worry about the first part. Cheating on your wife used to be called cheating on your wife. But then yuppies didn't like that name, on account of they think cheating is bad for some reason. So they changed it to open marriage. Which means you ain't cheating, you're just being open.

So be up front with your woman. Let her know that chicks dig you, and that by being into openness, you's just providing what you call your community service. If she squawks, tell her she's being selfish and setting a bad example for the young ones.

Besides, if you call it community service, the next time you get nailed on a burglary rap, you can bed down barmaids as part of your sentence.

Now about them blenders. You're right. There ain't what you call your good secondary market for small kitchen appliances. That's why when you send out the invitations, ask for handguns, power tools, and TVs. These is what sells best at pawnshops and bars.

Can I Still Wear White If I'm a Tramp?

Dear Dr. Verne:

I ain't exactly a virgin, and the priest knows, on the count of he's one of the guys who done stole my flower, if you hear what I'm saying.

Can I still wear white? Or do I gotta go with my second choice, which is lime green?

—Melva in Muncie

Dear Melva:

Going on color alone, I'd be thinking about your lime green anyways. Limes go good with gin and you can rub 'em under your arms when you ain't had time to bathe. You don't wanna get to stinking on your wedding night, otherwise your man might be figuring he'll sleep in the parking lot instead.

But if you're truly wedded to the white, I wouldn't go a worrying. The way I hear it, half the guys north of the Kentucky line done picked your flower, Melva. So if you was going by the virginity rules, you'd have to wear a funeral dress.

But the bright side is this: You ain't a looker. That means if anybody in the crowd got to pollinating you, he sure ain't fessing up to it.

Besides, what's the priest gonna say? According to priest rules, they's only supposed to sleep with altar boys. If he talks up about you, the guy's liable to get demoted to the Baptists, where they don't allow drinking and they're too cheap to even hire a pope.

Which Is Better Wedding Music: Mariah Carey or Molly Hatchet?

Dear Dr. Verne:

My woman's been planning out our wedding like we's some candy-ass rich people. Most of it I don't *mind, just so she leaves me outta it. But now she tells me she wants to have Mariah &%$#@#$ Carey music when we walk down the aisle. That's where I gotta draw the line.*

See, a lotta guys from the plant'll be there, and I don't wanna have 'em see me walking to no fruity music, on account of they'll think I'm gay, which means I'll probably get transferred to management.

I was thinking about a compromise, like that Molly Hatchet, who's nice and lovey and all, but still rocks. But she says that's more like confirmation music, and that if she can't have Mariah Carey, then she wants Whitney &%$#&% Houston. Are you kidding me? You gotta settle this, Verne.

—Mike in Atlanta

Dear Mike:

I'd say both of you's wrong. Weddings is basically boring as hell until you get to the drinking part. Ain't no music gonna fix that.

So if you don't wanna get transferred to management, make sure to hook the church up with a big screen over the altar. That way, while you're getting hitched, the boys from the plant could watch the Georgia–LSU game on big screen. Which means they won't start booing your ass if the vows take too long.

(Answers to all your important questions about varmint storage and drunk driving)

Now you being decent trash and all, you know you's a good parent. After all, it ain't *your* kids who's growed up to be perverts like that guy on Fox News, am I right?

That's cuz you's known to read quality self-help books, like this one you're spilling SpaghettiOs on right now, instead of them low-rent self-helps, which is always calling for tender nurturing and all that crap. You get to doing any of that nurturing, the next thing you know your kid's singing showtunes and wearing sparkly pants.

But seeing how you raised him right, he's probably sitting in jail as we speak. This here's what you call your teachable moment. Which means it's time to teach him the most basic lesson in life.

Choosing the Right Bail Bondsman

See, if he picks a bad one, he's gonna spend a lot more time in jail. Which means he ain't gonna be around to play wheelman for that Bed, Bath & Beyond robbery you was aiming to do.

Think of your bondsman as your best friend. Truth be told, he's actually better. Unlike your best friend, a bondsman will borrow you money.

It works like this: Say your kid gets caught burglarizing a plumbing and heating company. Now if he happened to get some of them Carrier Infinity central air units, I know a guy who'll buy 'em.

Anyways, the problem is he got caught. And seeing as how busting outta jail ain't real easy these days—they got pretty good food and TV, so why would a guy wanna leave?—you're gonna have to bail his ass out.

Enter the bondsman. For some money or collateral—which is stuff that got value, like a stuffed moose head or some cows—he will put up the bond for your kid's release. That means if he bolts for some of them greener pastures, like they got in West Virginia, the bondsman will have to pay off the court.

But this means the bondsman's also gonna be pissed. Which means he's gonna send a biker named Judas to beat your kid with towing chains and haul his ass back.

This here's what you call your foundation of a lasting, loving relationship.

Now there's one simple rule for choosing the right

bondsman: Make sure his name is manly sounding, like Mack, Frankie, Jesus, or Louie. Never hire a guy named Maurice or Oliver.

As you probably know from your own prison adventures, burglarizing a plumbing and heating company ain't real high on the criminal food chain. Your kid's gonna be in a holding cell with twenty guys who just decapitated their family. So you don't want to put him in no position where he's gotta say, "Guard, I must insist on speaking to Maurice immediately."

Them other twenty guys is gonna think he's calling for his interior decorator. That means they're either gonna stab him to death or, worse, make him talk about drapes.

But say his bondsman's name is Louie. Then he can say something manly like, "Yo, guard, I gotta get on the horn with Louie." Don't that sound better? It lets the other inmates know your boy hangs out with guys who got good criminal-sounding names. Which means they'll quit asking his thoughts on Berber carpeting.

It'll even get him a little status. So the next time one of them decapitators don't like the creamed corn the jail's serving for supper, he'll get the extra helping.

If You Can Trust Your Lawyer, He's an Amateur

The other main thing about parenting is making sure your kid got a good lawyer. You don't want him getting stuck with no guy from the public defender's office, on account of the guy probably isn't good at stealing, which is why he got a government job, on account of they got teachers.

If you ever watched Animal Planet or Court TV, you know lawyers is what you call your unique species. They're the only member of the reptile family who carries a briefcase.

Scientists figure lawyers is adaptable to all climates, as long as it got copy machines and white wine. Like wolves, lawyers survive by attacking the weakest in the herd—namely widows, CEOs, and other lawyers.

They also got what you call your highly developed mating system. When the male and the female lawyers meet, they don't climb naked into the shotgun seat of a Chevy Silverado, like decent people. They trade lies and paperwork, which done gives birth to baby lawyers, only they call 'em "billable hours."

Still, science guys ain't quite figured 'em out yet. Though lawyers look vaguely like real humans—except for them hairdos that got lacquered so much you figure they got a night job as an end table—they don't actually got a heart. When some lab-coat guys from Johns Hopkins once did an autopsy, all they could find in their guts was some child porn, three hundred grand in cash, and a one-way airline ticket to a country that got no extradition treaty.

All of which makes choosing the right lawyer damn hard.

Last thing you want is to show up in court, your kid's looking at three years for knocking off the Donutland, and all your lawyer talks about is due process and crap like that, instead of doing some quality lying, which is what you're paying him for.

That's why your ol' pal Verne done invented this test to make sure your kid's lawyer is a genuine scumbag, and not the artificial variety.

Testing Your Lawyer's Scumbagocity

1. Drop a nickel on the street. If your kid's lawyer dives for it, give him one point. If an old lady beats him to it, but he wrestles it away by punching her in the throat, give him two.

2. Say you're sitting at the bar during one of them delays where the judge goes golfing. Ask to hear the lawyer's favorite stories about defrauding crippled people. If he sits there thinking for a spell, then finally says, "Hmmm, there's just so many, I don't know where to start," give him one point.

3. Hire a dentist to look at his teeth. If they're sharp enough to bite through an iron stair rail, give him two points.

4. Instead of paying him in cash, ask if you can give him some rebuilt transmissions and a Hefty bag full of meth. If he smiles and says, "Yes, the resale opportunities at my daughter's elementary school would be quite promising," give him one point.

5. Ask the lawyer how many offspring he's eaten. ("Offspring," in case you ain't clued, is Chinese for "kids.") If he says, "I'm sorry, we only eat our young on special occasions, like Easter," he's not a dedicated professional. Knock off one point. But if he says, "Gawd, I haven't had

offspring in months. Do you know where I can score some?" give him one point.

6. If your kid's lawyer ever says the words "truth" or "justice," knock off six points and rat him out to the bar association.

The Scumbag Index

Now it's time to see if the lawyer is the kinda low-down skank who can get your kid probation, or if he mightta got born again and thinks God'll cut off his tongue if he tells more than sixteen lies per minute, which ain't enough for good lawyering.

Total the points and see where his Scumbag Index's at. This'll tell you what he's good for.

If he ain't good for nothing, try selling him to the Vietnamese. They eat carp. Which means they'll probably eat lawyer too if you was to sweeten the deal with a few packets of soy sauces.

7+

This here's a lawyer's lawyer, the kind who runs over little kids on the way to work just to get psyched up for the day. Give him six Hefty bags of meth and them bootleg Yo-Yo Ma tapes you ain't been able to unload, so he's always on retainer.

5–6

Your kid's lawyer only runs over stray cats and meter maids, but could probably handle misdemeanors and divorces.

3–4

The worthless bastard has only been indicted four times. He gets weird about embezzling from churches. Maybe you could let him wash you car, on account of a guy like this ain't gonna get too many lawyering jobs, and you'd only have to pay him a quarter cuz he wouldn't know better.

1–2

The guy does pro bono work, which is Latin for "I'm too dumb to send a bill." The last time he bribed a judge, he tried giving him six dollars and a pound cake. He hardly ever steals from the collection plate at Mass. He's about to get disbarred.

The Insensitive Man's Xmas Survival Guide

You're a man. Which means on the evolutionary scale, you's more advanced than a Chicago alderman, but way behind a pair of fishing waders.

Sure, you try to be sensitive. Like that time your kid was bawling cuz her guinea pig got ate by the German shepherd. You put your arm around her all comforting like and said, "Hey, kid, what's with the tears? I was thinking about eating that rat anyways. Probably go good with some mustard."

But you still caught hell. That's because White Trash being sensitive is like Leonardo DiCaprio winning a lumberjack competition. It ain't gonna happen.

Problem is, you got Christmas coming up. It's the most important time of year. If you nail this, every time you smash the car or get fired over the next twelve months, you can say to your woman, "Yeah, but remember that bracelet full of jewels I got you for Christmas?"

It don't matter you only paid thirteen bucks at the pawnshop and it's inscribed to "Leslie" when your woman's name is Charleen. It's the thought that counts.

The thing is, Christmas is the worst season for men. It's the time we gotta do some reflecting on the needs and wishes of others, which ain't our natural way.

But I also got some good news: They changed the rules of Christmas.

See, it used to be this celebration of Jesus, who they say was a damn good carpenter—even though he dressed like them fat ladies who stay in their nightgowns all day and watch TV. But then Jesus' in-laws grubbed on to the rights to Xmas and sold 'em to Halliburton.

Under the new Halliburton rules, they pretty much dropped all that caring crap and just made it a time to go broke buying presents.

Problem is, you still gotta fake like you care. See, most women ain't aware of the new rules. They still want you to be sensitive, like that fruity Hugh Grant. Which is why I got this five-point guide for faking your way through Christmas buying.

1. Avoid household appliances
Men is naturally attracted to these. They're large. They're

shiny. They got engines. But women don't see appliances as what you call your expression of love—except if they're German. They'll get to figuring you view them as unpaid maids. Your true feelings will be exposed.

2. Avoid power tools

Chances are your woman never whispered in a moment of tenderness, "Honey, if you really love me, you'd score me that ⁹⁄₁₆-inch chromium-plated drill bit I was always wanting." That's because women is weird; they don't understand the joys of hammering, sawing, puncturing, and blow torching stuff.

Fact is, giving your woman something real nice, like a radial arm saw or a rotary sander, could get your reproductive unit chopped off or, worse, make her donate your liquor cabinet to the Salvation Army.

3. Resist the old Bait & Switch

A lot of guys is powerless against the Bait & Switch Strategy. They're at Kmart and there it is, a brand-new Denver Nuggets sweatshirt or hunting overalls just your size. You know your woman ain't gonna score them for you. After all, women is always buying wuss stuff for Christmas, like sweaters with pictures of loons on 'em.

So you buy the sweatshirt and hunting pants for her, knowing they won't fit. Then you'll score 'em by default.

Problem is, we're men. We can outsmart kindergartners and bathroom fixtures, but not much else. Your woman will be onto you. And when you protest by saying,

"Honey, I always thought you looked like Demi Moore in size 38 camouflage pants," make sure there ain't no loaded weapons nearby.

4. Think volume

As a man, most of your brain is used for thinking about yourself. Fact is, outside eating and cable, there ain't much IQ left to consider anything else. That means you don't know what the hell your woman wants.

You can fix this by buying in volume. Instead of buying your woman one coat, buy eight in different colors. Chances are she won't like none of 'em, but she'll at least think you tried. You just happen to be pathetic.

Which is the great thing about women. They always cut you some slack for being pathetic. She'll expect less of you in the future, which is way better than having her like what you got her.

5. Buy lots of worthless crap

Since men ain't got the mechanical requirements for an imagination, we usually go for worthless gifts. Like winter boots, clothesline poles, a rear-window defroster.

But don't expect your woman to turn to you on Christmas morning with moist eyes and say, "Oh, honey, new rain gutters!"

Most people want worthless stuff for Christmas. You know, like jewelry, opera tickets, and them imported cheeses from Tennessee. The goal is to give them junk they'd never buy.

That's because in America, the best way to show your love is to waste your money on someone else.

Lessons on Winning Bar Fights, Scoring Points with the Boss's Wife, and Drunk Driving During the White Trash Social Season

Now seeing as how this here book's about etiquette, which is French for "don't be an asshole," we best get to discussing the finer points to acting proper during the White Trash social season, which begins with the first beer at kickoff on New Year's Day, and usually ends when you done passed out in a Dumpster behind the fish market on December 31.

See, most people figure parties is times of good cheer. You're supposed to get together with friends, family, and coworkers, celebrate them good fortunes, and be thankful you ain't a U.S. senator or got your arm mauled by a wolverine.

But to White Trash, parties is loaded up with what you call your dangerous perils. All the things known to go wrong for our people—open bars and romantic interludes in the parking lot of a Holiday Inn—is all under one roof. If you never cheated on your husband or blowed chow on the best shoes of the foreman's wife, this here's your opportunity.

Now I ain't saying I can help you get outta this alive. But if you do it right, you could probably get through with just a suspended sentence and a good place in line at the liver transplant clinic.

Tips for Dressing Proper

Now there's two kinds of parties—the kind with kin or your buddies, and the kind where you might be called to fancy up for a spell.

The first kind don't call for no dressing up. Hell, if it's at your sister-in-law's house, you probably don't need no clothes at all, seeing as how she's looser than the tranny of an '87 Yugo.

But say you got your special occasion. Maybe it's a pre-sentencing affair for your brother's three-strikes conviction. Maybe the treasurer down at the Teamsters hall just beat a RICO case. Or maybe profits is up 129 percent this year, so your boss is finally gonna throw you an Xmas party, seeing as how it's way cheaper than giving you a raise.

Your woman is gonna be pumped. It's that one time of year when she gets to wear the fancy dress she got from Sears for your cousin's fifth wedding back in '93. Okay, so maybe she put on ten or twenty pounds since then. Hell, maybe it was fifty if your stump-grinding business is going good and you got extra money for Stovetop Stuffing.

But there ain't nothing finer than a woman in a tight black dress, even if she is your wife.

Problem is, that means you gotta dress up too. Try jaking outta this all you want, but your woman's gonna be pissed if you figure on wearing your Carhartts and a Chicago Bears hat.

Give in on this point. From where I'm sitting, you're gonna get in a lot bigger trouble before the night's done, so's you might as well score some points early.

Think about some nice flannel that got no blood on it from field dressing deers, maybe your Marlboro jacket, and your best steel-toes—the ones that got no bearing grease on 'em.

This, friends, is what you call class.

The Torture of Mingling

Mingling is the worst part of any fancy party. In case you didn't know, it's Ojibwe for "I'd rather eat a rich lady's china cupboard than yap with you."

When you first get there, everybody's acting like one big happy family, which they ain't, and like everybody cares about everybody, which they don't. So if it's a work party, that means you gotta mingle till you naturally separate into bosses, white-collar guys, and decent working people, at which point you can start getting hammered.

But be careful. This is the one time of year the boss acts human. That means he might talk to you.

He's gonna want to meet your woman, ask about the family, tell your wife how good of a worker you is, even though he only pays $6.40 an hour and thinks your name is Harry.

You also gotta make an impression on the boss' wife. A few tips for scoring in this situation: Try not to talk about fan belts, drinking the worms in tequila, or the burglary you did at that hair replacement clinic.

She being a rich lady and all, you gotta talk refined. Try saying some deep and thoughtful stuff like, "The Cavaliers ain't gonna be &%$# this year if LeBron don't start hitting the three," or "You know any decent places for trout fishing around here?"

This is what you call subtle. Rich folks is impressed by that. Next thing you know, she'll be telling the old man how refined you is, you get promoted to foreman, and next time your woman needs a dress, you got the jack to score one from someplace really classy, like Target.

The Respectful Guest Always Brings a Gift

Okay, so say your kid goes on a meth bender and ends up proposing by accident to some rich girl from one of them places called Barrington Woods Estates. You figure she's a skank, on account of she don't like Hank Williams Jr., but the missus says you gotta go to the engagement party the girl's folks is throwing. Besides, it won't be that bad; rich people always got good TVs.

Anyways, you gotta bring a gift. It's the international sign for saying, "Hey, thanks for letting me come over and drink up all your liquor."

Now it don't matter if it's a wake, an anniversary, or you're doing a home invasion robbery and you wanna show a little class—me, I always wrap up a hockey stick. It's good for unclogging gutters, pushing your kids outta the way of the TV, or beating your neighbors who squawk about all the broke snowmobiles in your front yard. You can also use it to hold up vines in your tomato patch or hunt deer when you're too broke for ammo.

So while everybody else is bringing them dainty little pen sets or some goddamned fruit baskets—What? Do they figure the host got sired by some guys from the marsupial family?—you'll be the only guy showing real class.

Danger! Open Bar Ahead!

There comes a time in every trash's life when he's confronted by something so big, so menacing, that there's no turning back. Yep, I'm talking about the open bar.

(At this point, it woulda been good to cue the ominous music, like they do in movies, which tells you some scary-ass scenes is coming up. I was thinking Mushroomhead or Slipknot might be good. But seeing as how Broadway Books is too cheap to spring for a soundtrack, on account of they probably spent all their money on scones and venti, which is rich people food that got no meat in it, just pretend some scary music got played right here.)

Putting an open bar in front of White Trash is like throwing a batch of naked cheerleaders into the prison exercise yard. You're in trouble. I ain't even gonna advise you on this on account of you'll be in a coma by morning, so's you won't be able to thank me. But I got some suggestions:

1. Belly up to a crowded part of the bar. When you pass out, you'll land on someone else first, instead of going straight to the floor and smacking your head too hard.

2. If you gotta barf, do it with class. Never barf on the

bar. Just bend down so no one sees, barf, then throw somebody else's coat on top of it. Nobody's the wiser, and the bartender won't cut you off.

3. Once you got about nine or fourteen shots in you, anything with two legs is gonna be looking fine. But don't go pawing at the waitress. This also gets you cut off. Make sure you paw at the wife of a buddy who's littler than you. Which leads us to . . .

Nothing Better Than a Good Brawl

According to section 4.32 of the White Trash Constitution, "Any party, wedding, funeral, or holiday gathering must include at least one brawl. Catfights or stomping parking lot attendants do not fulfill this requirement."

Which is why it's your sacred duty to do a little knuckling.

Just remember: It ain't your fault. It's the fault of whoever got the bright idea to spring for an open bar. Moron shoulda knowed better.

Now it's always a good idea to pick on little guys. Whisky don't taste good if your mouth is bleeding. Little guys usually punch you in the stomach or neck, which don't cut into your drinking ability.

But make sure you win. If you get your ass whupped by the midget whose wife you was pawing at, most guys'll figure you're a cross-dresser or a Dodgers fan. So if you're too hammered and might lose, fake like you're having a pancreas failure. Your buddies won't know what that is. They'll give you shots of Beam to make it better. And nobody'll punch you out for at least a year, on account of they don't wanna catch no pancreas failure, too.

Bonus Round for the Ladies

Okay, ladies, so say you're at the company party, and your old man has ignored you all night. Now he's back to pawing at the midget's wife. That means you got diplomatic immunity to do some tomcatting yourself—and finally score a decent man.

My advice: Do the old Heaving Chest Maneuver on one of them front-office guys.

Two things you gotta know about white-collar fruities: First off, they're part girl, so you gotta check to make sure they're capable of reproducting activity.

Second off, they got the romantic powers of a smoked muskie. But at least they're into that sensitive stuff, which means they'll think it's therapeutic if you get drunk and start talking about poisoning your husband with some Weed-B-Gone.

Of course, the front-office guy's trophy wife is gonna be pissed. Don't worry. You could whup her two days from Hell on account of all she eats is SlimFast and celery. Besides, she'll be ascared you'll put bruises on her, which won't match her jogging suit when she's power walking at the mall.

When the trophy wife ain't looking, drag Mr. Fruity into a supply closet. Once he gets a taste of that good trash, he ain't going back.

And if he's gonna keep the affair going, he's gonna have

to schedule your old man for overtime to get him outta the house. That puts you in the bonus round: You got an extra man on the side, and there's more overtime money for scoring Lean Cuisine.

The Best Way to Drunk Drive Is in Someone Else's Car

Once it gets past ten, the bosses and the white collars usually go home, on account of they can't hold their liquor and gotta jog on their NordicTracks. Which means for the next few hours the decent people got the bar to themselfs. Which means you can brawl, have domestic arguments, and wreck stuff.

But sooner or later the dainty little %$#@ with the bow tie behind the bar, who's probably working his way through law school so's he can sue grandmas and orphans, is gonna call it closing time.

Enter your biggest problem of the night: drunk driving. Seeing as how your woman took the truck to meet Mr. Wussification at the Holiday Inn, you either gotta walk it, hitch it, or catch a ride.

But the smart trash knows there's another option. See, you figured the evening would go like this. You'd get hammered, your woman would get pissed, she'd take off with a white-collar fruity, and you'd be stuck hoofing it. Which is why she drove your truck, and you borrowed your buddy's.

The best way to drunk drive is always in someone else's car. Say you end up careening through a Pontiac dealership, or you figure you're gonna park in the showroom of a pet store. You're gonna be too hung over in the morning to deal with it. Which means you don't want your name on the title, on account of it's way better if the cops come looking for your buddy instead.

If a major accident happens, just abandon the truck, hitch a ride home, and tell your buddy it was stolen.

After all, he's your buddy, ain't he? He shouldn't mind giving of himself so the truly needy can sleep off an open bar. Ain't that what friendship is all about?

All that talk about open bars is making me thirsty. Which means we gotta change the subject, otherwise I'll be bolting down to McCarthy's, where they got one-dollar beers and the waitress sneaks you shots of Jameson if you bum her cigs.

Which means I won't be coming back. Which means I'll never finish this goddamned book. Which means I'll probably have to end it with a whole bunch of blank pages and call it performance art.

Problem is, my editor is from the Silicon Valley, where they's known for making fake boobs. And it ain't gonna look too good if I'm all beat up in the bread line at St. Malachi's tomorrow, and I gotta explain that I almost got pummeled to death by some fake boobs.

Which means we gotta stop talking about liquor and get to the other most important part about home life: dogs and varmints.

Really, Eunice, I Thought That Dog Was a Minnow

Dear Dr. Verne:

My wife finally flipped. She went out and bought one of them high-dollar fluffy yip dogs. You know, the kind you use to clean out your shotgun? Now I know what you're thinking: "Why don't you just be a man and put your foot down, you big sissy?" But ya see, Verne, Eunice is one fine piece of woman. When this woman wears spandex, there isn't one man who don't turn his head. So I needs to know how to tell her that the dog has to go diplomatic like.

—Bob in Quincy, Illinois

Dear Bob:

You don't gotta tell me Eunice is stepping dynamite. I seen her do karaoke at the Viking Lounge before. If it wasn't for that big scar on her cheek, she could get a job at Hooters.

But women is funny about them fufu dogs. I don't know how you're gonna tell her it's either you or the dog without you being the one staying at Motel 6.

Me, I'd lie.

Now most self-help guys will tell you lying ain't good. But they ain't married to Eunice.

My advice is to take the dog hunting and leave it out in a field, then tell your woman he ran away. If that don't work—seeing as how

fluff dogs ain't easy to drag outta the car—then I'd use it for walleye bait. Just tell Eunice you mistaked it for a large minnow and that you're terribly sorry and that's why you bought her this black Lab to make up for it.

As I recall, Eunice may be USDA-inspected Grade-A meat, but she ain't no master mechanic upstairs.

Newlywed Varmint Storage Problems

Dear Dr. Verne:

Each winter my friend Jeff has been trapping coon and storing them in the freezer until he had enough to sell. (The buyer don't want Jeff skinnin' 'em 'cause he ain't very good at it.) Now that Jeff got married, things changed.

His wife spotted a frozen paw sticking out of a garbage bag and resting on a leftover wedding cake she'd saved. She made him remove the coons and then she threw out the cake.

Jeff can't store the coons outside 'cause the dogs eat them, or it warms up too much and they bloat. His mom lives down the road and lets him use her freezer, but it's a small one and filled up fast. He even asked me if I got any extra fridge space.

Seems to me he ought to solve this problem back home instead of shipping coons out across the county. What's your thoughts on this?

—Concerned on the Mesabi Range

Dear Mesabi Range Guy:
Jeff gotta lay down the law, only it ain't as easy as it used to be.

Back in the old days, a guy could tell his woman how it was gonna be, and she'd listen. Hell if I know why. It just was.

But now they got this marital equality. That means you got what they call shared responsibilities, which is the fruity way of saying men don't got it good no more.

Me, I ain't exactly partial to it, on account of in the old days all we had to do is howl and drink and forget to pick stuff up from the grocery store. Why be a moron and give that up?

But under this shared responsibility, you gotta divide the bossing evenly.

Take Jeff's wife. She oughtta be in charge of cooking, cleaning, and tending after the kids and money, on account of women don't drink up paychecks as much.

Jeff, he should be the boss of fixing stuff, shooting at the stray pit bulls, and saying where the dead coons is stored.

Problem is, Jeff's wife is probably one of them feminisms who gone to college. She's looking to get say over the freezer, too, so she can expand her sphere of influence, which is military talk for saying Jeff's about to get his ass kicked.

That's why most decent trash get a little

something going on the side. Business guys call this finding an auxiliary supplier. If Jeff was to score himself a side honey—I hear there's a woman at the Mountain Iron bait shop who's loose—then he'd also score an extra coon-storing facility.

But what I'm really thinking about is that wedding cake. You know where Jeff's old lady tossed it? I wouldn't mind you sending me a piece if you could find it.

Is It Okay to Shoot My Neighbor?

Dear Dr. Verne:

I got a problem. It seems that my neighbor in the blue trailer (you know, the one with no roof) has been parking his Pinto in my driveway. This makes me mad 'cause I just done laid new gravel and I ain't got to use it yet.

I asked the preacher what I should do about it, and he said I should share (mostly cause I don't have a car anyway), but I don't wanna share.

What I want to know is this: Can I shoot him, or should I put a certain yellow bodily fluid in his still?

By the way, can you get sick by drinking varnish?

—Arnie in Savannah, Georgia

Dear Arnie:
Your first mistake was talking to that preacher,

who wasn't even good enough to get into the Priest Union, so he had to become a preacher, who don't even say Mass, just some cheap-ass services.

But the preacher's right about one thing: A guy should share. It's okay to share stuff like pry bars or Pall Malls or the leftover ham your woman cooked in April, seeing as how it's green now anyways.

But driveways is a different story. It says so right in the White Trash Constitution: "Thou shalt not covet they neighbor's wife or driveway." Which means the guy in the blue trailer's probably a Satan worshipper.

In most states it's okay to shoot Satan worshippers, just so's you wait till hunting season and don't bag over your limit. But I don't figure the point of putting yellow bodily fluid in his still.

First off, it's against the Sacred White Trash Ways to wreck a batch of liquor. Think about all the starving children in Africa who coulda drank it.

Second off, if you got yellow bodily fluids seeping outta you, I'd get your ass to a doctor. It sounds like your radiator might be leaking, and if your heart don't get enough coolant, it'll probably blow up and get guts all over your good recliner.

Now about the varnish. It says on the label

you ain't supposed to drink it, but that's just sissy talk made up by pointy-head scientists who can't hold their liquor or their industrial wood treatments.

I say it's okay to drink, but it's better when you mix it with some OJ and gin.

I Cheated on My Cousin and Killed My Uncle's Bird Dog

Dear Dr. Verne:

You gotta help me! I was at a family reunion at my Uncle Billy's place when it all happened. My cousin Marly caught me in the bedroom naked with his wife. She started it.

Anyways, while I was taking the gun away from him, it went off. The slug went through the floor of the trailer and killed my uncle's bird dog.

Now my wife is mad at me and I ain't getting any. Besides that, I ain't got three hundred bucks for no new bird dog. Everybody's mad at me. What should I do?

—New Hampshire White Trash

Dear New Hampshire Trash:

First off, fighting with your relatives is what separates us trash from your lesser class of people, like what they got in Hollywood. When they fight with each other, they hire up some fruit boy lawyer with them oval-shaped glasses to throw paperwork at each other. Decent

people, they try to shoot each other, on account of it's cheaper.

But I'd be thinking about getting some new lies when you get caught naked. Me, I never had much luck with the she-started-it excuse.

The first trick is to pretend like you're a doctor and you're doing one of them mammograms, which is this test doctors thought up so's they could feel their customers' boobs. But since it's a big French word, husbands won't know what the hell you're talking about. Which means they'll get their ass outta there right quick on account of they don't wanna catch no French stuff.

But say you're dealing with a smarter than normal husband, like maybe he's a union steward or something. That means you go to stage two: Pretend like you didn't know she was married.

Of course, your cousin ain't gonna buy this, on account of you was at the wedding. But just tell him you was hammered that day, and that you thought you was romping with your own woman. He's bound to cut you some slack, on account of this probably happened to him before, too.

The bird dog thing is more serious. Since you ain't got the three hundred, I'd try trading your uncle something of equal value, like your life-size pheasant statue that doubles as a cig lighter. That's gotta be worth a couple thousand, seeing as how it's art. Your uncle could probably trade it to some yuppies for their SUV, then everybody's happy.

How to Score with Bob and Impress Human Services

Dear Dr. Verne:

I found me a real good man. His name is Bob. He was working on the construction site near my office. One day I was outside for my smoke break and we got to talking.

Then his union went on strike, so we spent about a week doing the bone dance in my trailer. It was all romantic and stuff, but then they settled the strike. Human Services brought back my kids about the same time.

Since then, I haven't been able to get no quality time with Bob. I ain't opposed to locking the young ones outside on a nice day for a couple of seconds, but with all this damn rain, they keep tracking mud on my green shag carpet and I have to wipe down my plastic furniture covers. Any suggestions?

—Searchin' for Solitude in Massachusetts

Dear Searchin':

You got what them pointy-heads call your parental dilemma. You can't be locking the kids out too long, on account of the neighbors will rat you to Human Services, who'll send your kids to live with them yuppies, who'll teach 'em not to shoot their 12-gauge at the rats in the house, which means they'll be wrecked by the time you get 'em back.

Then again, a fine lady like you deserves to get her bone dancing in with Bob.

What you need is a toolshed.

Whenever I have Velvet or Sherry or Honey Bee over while the old lady's working the graveyard shift, I send the kids to the toolshed. I give 'em a bag of Marshmallow Mateys and tell 'em there's five bucks in it if they can shut up and pretend they're playing in a crack house with no electricity.

Seeing as how five bucks can buy a lot of cigs or a pawnshop buck knife, the kids is happy to obey. That way they stay dry, so's they ain't dragging no mud in the house, and I got plenty of time to play jackhammer with them afore-mentioned ladies.

But say you ain't got no toolshed. Me, I'd think about locking 'em in one of the Trans Ams you got on blocks in the front yard. Tell 'em it's a spaceship, and if they get out before you come back, their eyes'll get burnt up and they won't be able to watch *SpongeBob* no more. That'll teach 'em.

And if your old man happened to take the

Trans Ams with him when he left, which ain't likely, Bob can make himself useful and dig a dry hole under the trailer. Tell the kids to play army and pretend it's a foxhole. Then toss a few firecrackers out the window from time to time to make it seem authentic.

This is what pointy-heads call nurturing their creativity. Human Services will be impressed.

Todd's Big Tornado Scam

Dear Dr. Verne:

During the last tornado at my trailer court, me and my wife, Lorlene, were only able to get six out of seven of our kids into the culvert. The tornado picked up Travis, our ten-year-old, who was making a run for the woods. The damn thing dropped him in a nearby farmer's sorghum field.

Now this farmer hates me cuz I'm always fishin' his pond without his okay. So he recognizes Travis as my kid and turns him over to the county social services department and starts ranting about child neglect. The local press picked up on it and showed a lot of video of Travis limping around with all these bruises and bandages.

Now, Verne, I know Travis and I know his fake limp. He's milking this for all it's worth. The whole county is treating him like a king.

I'm mighty proud of him. There's even some old

rich couple who wants to adopt him. This couple would probably die soon after, and Travis and his real family would be set for life.

My problem is Lorlene misses Travis and wants to fight to get him back. Me, I'm loving the extra room in the trailer and next week I could save $3 when I take the family to the drive-in for our summer vacation.

Verne, what should I do?

—*Todd in Tulsa*

Dear Todd:

You and the missus oughtta be right proud the way you raised that boy. There ain't a lotta kids these days who will milk a leg injury for the sake of their family.

But you gotta do something about the missus. First off, it's her job to think about what's best for the family. If she'd do one of them cost-benefit analysises, which is how rich guys figure money stuff out, she'd know it's way better economics to have Travis soaking them elderlies instead of mooching off you.

Second off, tell her to quit bawling about missing the kid. Hell, he's only ten. She'll have plenty a time to see him when them old folks die, you get rich, and all you gotta do is sit on the porch, swill Beam, and watch the drunk drivers ram the train bridge.

Fact is, I ain't seen my two oldest in three

years, ever since they got caught trying to rob that dermatologist in Nebraska. But you don't hear my woman squawking. That's because she knows if them two's in prison, they ain't at home snarfing up all the Captain Crunch and liquor.

(You're gonna thank
me next time you're
in a bar and you find
yourself rooting for
some hairdressers
from L.A.)

CHAPTER VI

RECREATION

Sports is the religion of the White Trash. Only it's better cuz they got it on TV at bars and they don't mooch for money without giving you a beer.

But some people—mainly them TV fruities with the five-quart mousse jobs—get to defiling the name of the Cleanup Hitter in the Sky by saying them dainty games is sports. So let ol' Verne clue you on what's right, and what will get you sent to the Burning Lake of Fire.

Tips on What Sports Is Good and What Sports Is for Guys Named Chauncey

Those of you who got Catechism probably recognize this from Corinthians: "And on the Seventh Day, God figured

He was already in deep &%$# for violating the union rules. So He declared it a day of rest to keep OSHA off His ass.

" 'Kick back,' He told all the guys in the shop. 'Have yourself a couple of brewskies, just so long as it ain't none of them designer beers from Europe. And for chrissakes don't be watching no fruity sports. You start watching tennis and the next thing you know everybody wants to be in management and we got nobody to run the jack-hammers.' "

But like a lot of things, people got to thinking the word of God was optional. Now it threatens what you call your very existence of the once proud White Trash Nation.

Here's a handy guide to keep you in the good graces of God. Games is rated on a 1 to 10 Manliness Scale.

NASCAR: 9

Racing's got engines and noise, which is manly. It also got tow trucks and crashes and explosions and fire. But can't somebody figure out how to get some grenade launchers into this bad boy? You put some heavy artillery on the hood of Dale Jr.'s car, and they'll finally start showing NASCAR on primetime, instead of shows about guys named Scooter sucking up to Donald Trump.

This woulda got a 10, except they let Jeff Gordon in.

Baseball: 8

The most drunk-friendly game. Since nothing ever happens, you can get hammered, fall out of the bleachers, crack your melon open, go to the emergency room, get twenty-three stitches, barhop your way back to the stadium, and not miss a batter.

Basketball: 7

At this point you're probably saying, "What gives, Verne? That guy Dennis Rodman got a red hairdo and wears dresses. And basketball got cute little matching outfits, just like tennis."

You got yourself a point here. Basketball's got too many skinny guys, like they might be vegetarians. And them baggy shorts? Hell, why don't they just make 'em plaid and call it fratball? The first guy to drink two beers, get punched out, and throw up on a sorority chick wins.

But at least basketball also got a lotta manly talk in it. You never hear no tennis announcer say, "Steffi Graf thunders into the paint and RIPS DOWN THE TOMA-HAWK JAM!"

Boxing: 3

Boxing used to be a sport. But then they got to charging for it on Pay-Per-View. God got pissed.

Corinthians 12:02: "And then God found out if He wanted to catch the Holyfield–Tyson fight, He was gonna have to spring fifty-nine bucks on Pay-Per-View. God announced a boycott.

" 'Next guy around here who orders Pay-Per-View gets his ass personally kicked by God,' He said. Though Paul figured he could whup God—seeing as how God wasn't exactly buff, on account of He spent most of His time laying on the couch bossing people around—none of the disciples wanted to risk their cushy patronage jobs. And so it was decreed."

Figure Skating: 1
Guys named Boris prancing around in ballerina costumes to public radio music. There's no checking. No penalties. You never see 'em drop the gloves and duke it out with them other fruities in ballerina costumes. And I'll be damn sure you never heard nobody at the bar say, "I'll lay $50 and take the 6 points on the wuss in the pink outfit."

Football: 10
Fat guys smashing into each other in space uniforms. Almost as good as a Bruce Willis movie. All that's missing is the T&A and explosions.

Golf: –3
Here you got a bunch of guys named Lance and Chauncey. They're wearing matching pastel outfits and riding around in go-carts. They ain't even cool go-carts, with dual exhausts or nothing. They're them plastic ones old men use for fetching groceries in Arizona.

Hockey: 11
The official sport of the White Trash. Nothing better than toothless guys trying to filet each other with unsharpened lumber. The only problem is you can't pronounce their names, on account of half of 'em got drunk and spent their vowels on hookers and tattoos.

Olympics: 1

Gymnastics? Midget fourteen-year-olds boinging around on a mattress.

Skiing? Get a snowmobile, pal.

Diving? I could show you twenty guys in powder blue tuxes jumping into a Best Western pool at a wedding reception. But they don't put it on ESPN and call it a sport. It's called twenty drunks falling in the water.

Bicycling? If your car got repossessed and you're stuck riding a bike, be a man, get a job or rob a 7-Eleven and earn for yourself. But don't think cuz you're broke you can call it a sport. If that was true, sitting on the steps drinking forty-ounce Millers at 11.00 a.m. on a Wednesday would be a sport, too.

Soccer: 1

You ever heard of England? It used to be this big country that captured all these extra countries around the world. Then the English started playing soccer. Pretty soon they got so dainty they was getting their ass kicked by India, which got an army about as good as Iowa's.

Tennis: 1

It beats the hell outta me why people wanna see them little foreigners hit a fuzzy ball. You can almost hear their mas yelling, "Don't get your clothes dirty before the regatta, Skippy."

They even got a fruity way of keeping score. Six-love. Sounds like a sex line. "Call 1-900-6-LOVE and talk to

Skippy, Biff, and Douglas, three naughty little probate at-
torneys waiting to fulfill your hottest dreams."

How to Keep from Getting Your Ass Kicked at Sports Bars in Wisconsin

Nothing causes bad luck faster than rooting for sissy
teams. Guys see you at a sports bar, pounding wine cool-
ers and yelling for a team with effeminate qualities, they
got no choice but to take you out back and beat you with
a cardboard Old Style display. It's White Trash law.

Take the guy who shows up at a Stevens Point, Wisconsin, bar with a Drew Henson jersey on. First off, he
ain't gonna get no chicks. Decent ladies know "Dallas" in
Cambodian means, "I get my ass beat at arm-wrestling by
bank tellers."

That's the bad luck I'm trying to clue you about.

There's basically three ways to avoid getting your ass
kicked in a sports bar.

1. Don't Root for Nobody from the South

When people think White Trash, they think South. Folks
is always confusing us for them rednecks, who's different,
on account of they got no teeth and play banjos and look
like their ma was a zoo animal.

But there's a big difference between your quality White
Trash and your garden variety inbred.

See, us trash is more behaved. When we date our
cousins, at least we take 'em out for dinner and buy 'em
something pretty before we get to having babies.

But people still get confused, which is why you don't usually wanna root for no southern teams, unless they got really manly sounding names.

Say the foreman sees you rooting for the Florida Marlins. Now in case you ain't clued in, Marlins is a big fish with a long, pointy horn. But your foreman, he's used to fishing for quality, like your walleye and what have you. So he thinks Marlin is that magician on TV. And everyone knows magicians is practically mimes.

Which means if he sees you rooting for mimes, he'll get to figuring you got the IQ of a belt sander. Which means he's gonna assign you to mopping the hazardous waste room, on account of you won't know better.

2. Don't Root for Fruities from Southern California

The guy gets home from work every day at 6:00 p.m., slips out of his cute yellow sweater and his Dockers, cranks up some Yanni, and sits on the couch, careful not to get crumples on his fuchsia jogging suit.

"Honey," he says to his woman, "I had a hard day at the computer factory, lifting them heavy computer chips and all. Could you please get me a designer water with a lemon twist?"

That's why you don't root for nobody from Southern California. Next to France and Melrose Place, there ain't no place sissier.

Everybody in Southern California is either a advertising guy, a computer geek, or has fake blond hair and talks like he was in that movie *The Birdcage*. You ever see a guy from California chop a cord of wood with only an ax and a sixer of Pigs Eye?

Say you go to that bar in Stevens Point dressed like a Californian. You got your man-purse, your cute little Hawaii shirt, and about seventeen pounds of hair gel. The smart money says you get your ass whupped before you pound your first wine spritzer—even if there's only old men and cripples at the bar.

What happens the next day when you show up at the plant, and all the guys is wanting to know what happened? If you gotta say, "I was rooting too loud for the Lakers and got my ass whupped by a quadriplegic," expect to get reassigned to hazardous waste storage by noon.

3. But What If a Southern Team with a Sissy Name Is Playing Them Candy-Asses from Southern California?

Here's where the figuring gets hard. On one hand, you got your inbreds. On the other, you got fruities who'd rather be watching Barbra Streisand on Pay-Per-View.

So you go with the tiebreaker: whichever name sounds the manliest.

Say Duke is playing USC. Duke sounds like a bunch of tea-sipping fruities from England who got wigs and tights. "Cheeves, I seem to have misplaced my spectacles."

USC is named the Trojans, which used to be an army from Greece or someplace like that. Since armies is manlier than cross-dressers, go with USC.

But that ain't true if you're watching, say, Florida–UCLA. This time, the southerners is named after a Gator, which bites people and makes good cowboy boots.

The Southern Californians is named after a Bruin, which most people call bears. But if he was a real bear, he wouldn't be living in California cuz the only thing to eat in the garbage is tofu and low-fat yogurt. That's why they call him Bruin, which in bear language means, "I got an appointment with my hairstylist at three."

But say you got the worst of all cases: The Anaheim Mighty Ducks is playing the Dallas Stars.

One team's named after a movie that didn't have no explosions. The other's named after some actresses who spend all their time in tanning booths and getting electrolysis.

At this point, slowly back away, turn off the TV, and burn your clothes. You don't want none of that getting contagious on you.

Teams That Will Jinx You So You Won't Even Be Able to Grow a Decent Beard, Like That Dainty Ethan Hawke

1. Alabama Crimson Tide
Named after red laundry soap. What happens when they get tackled and their pants get dirty? Does their moms come down and pull their ears?

2. Philadelphia Phillies

I like chicks just as much as the next guy, but I wouldn't name no baseball team after them. Next thing you know, a pitcher is getting shelled in the middle of the fourth inning, and the manager stops the game to talk about his feelings.

3. Georgia Tech Yellow Jackets

The only people who wear yellow jackets is Hollywood fruities and old ladies on Easter. If they're gonna have a sissified name, they should do it right and call themselves the Georgia Tech Boutonnieres, which is French for, "I got a flower stuck on my jacket."

4. Orlando Magic

Ain't this cute. Little fairies with batons prancing around putting spells on princesses. You think a fairy's gonna go to the boards with Amare Stoudemire?

5. Los Angeles Clippers

Clippers is what hairdressers call their scissors. Only L.A. would name their team after a hairdresser shop.

6. Jacksonville Jaguars

Named after a rich man's car. That's soooo scary. *Don't be coming into our house, boy, or we gonna get all climate-control seating on yo ass.*

7. San Diego Chargers

See what I was saying about them So-Cals? One town names their team after hairdressers, and the other names it after trophy wives who get to firing up their American Express like its free ammo night at the gun range.

8. Stanford Cardinal

This here's a rich kids' school, but they're only called the Cardinal, like they couldn't afford more than one. You ever been to Baltimore? It looks like it got firebombed in a Teamsters strike. But they still got enough class to spring for more than one Oriole.

Here's a tip, rich kids: If your pa done cut off your allowance, stick a couple beers in your pocket so it looks like you got a gun, and head down to the pet store. Then say to the clerk, "Hey pal, hand me over a batch of cardinals, or the iguana gets it." This is how decent people get to putting S's on the end of their names. Ain't them professors teaching you none of them supplies and demand?

9. Utah Jazz

Named after music where guys screech on trumpets so it sounds like you're in a traffic jam. Believe it or not, yuppies pay to hear this, when they coulda just walked on the freeway at suppertime for free.

10. South Carolina Gamecocks

Ol' Verne likes to play hide the salami as much as the next trash, but you don't wanna name your team after no manly reproduction apparatus, if you hear what I'm saying. It's gonna attract the kinda lady who don't got all her shots. Which means you're gonna have to soak your manlies in turpentine to get rid of whatever she's gonna give you.

The Ten Manliest Teams

1. Minnesota Vikings
The manliest team of all, on account of they're named after guys who used to ride around in boats, kick the %$#@ outta Scotsmen for wearing dresses, and steal all their liquor and women.

2. Green Bay Packers
It ain't glamorous, but trash who's been evicted a decent amount knows the value of a good packer. Especially if you don't got enough money for a U-Haul and got to fit everything in the skimpy-assed box of a Chevy S-10.

3. Colorado Buffaloes
Okay, so they ain't much sport for hunting. But they're big, furry, and they got them ZZ Top beards. You can tell they're the union stewards of the animal kingdom by the way they stand around doing nothing.

4. Milwaukee Brewers
Makers of the sacred nectar. From what you call your religious perspective, they're probably the fifth most important deity in the Universe after God, Jesus, the Virgin

Mother, and bail bondsmen. Don't root for these guys and the smart money says St. Peter smokes your ass before you get a word in edgewise.

5. North Dakota Fighting Sioux
Named after guys who didn't have jobs and just rode around hunting and fighting for the hell of it. Think of 'em as the olden days' version of bikers, only they dressed like them guys from *Pocahontas* and didn't have to worry about burning oil in their horses.

6. Providence Friars
Nothing tastes better than when it got cooked in a batch of burning fat. Toss in some bologna and maybe a bone or two if you can get 'em away from the dog, and you're looking at some good eating.

Hell, once when I was broke, I even fried up a catcher's mitt for supper. It was a might bit chewy, but the kids said it was better than them vegetables we made 'em eat one time.

7. Maryland Terrapins
These is what most folks know as turtles. But seeing as how this is a college, they had to give it a fancier name, on account of rich people won't pay twenty grand a year to send their kid to turtle-catching school.

According to *Webster's Dictionary*, turtles is mostly found in "brackish waters." I ain't never been to Brackish, so's I usually just get 'em at the pond or when they're laying eggs in the asphalt. But make sure you throw 'em in the fryer before you eat 'em. My pal Donny once tried to eat a snapper before it got fried. The damn thing bit off his lips, so now he's gotta drink beer through his nose.

8. North Carolina Tar Heels

This here's a good working man's name. It shows that when your team ain't playing football, it's doing manly labor and get all dirty, which chicks dig. If they was to call themselves the North Carolina Paper Cuts, chicks wouldn't dig 'em.

9. Arkansas Razorbacks

I'm figuring the guy who named 'em musta done time, on account of getting stabbed in the back with a razor ain't something a guy's prone to forgetting. My woman once caught me with her sister when I was supposed to be out tomcatting with her aunt, which my woman didn't mind on account of her aunt looks like a forklift. Anyways, after I passed out, the missus carved her name in my back with one of them Bic razors, just so's I would remember I was married, which means I'm supposed to get her okay before having affairs.

Calling your team the Razorbacks is a good way of not forgetting this.

10. Indianapolis Colts

This here's what you call your double score: Named after both a gun and a forty-ouncer of malt liquor, which always go good together.

The Manly Man's Guide to Vehicles: A Scientific Study

Priests will tell you that man was started by Adam, that moron from the Garden of Eden.

I ain't buying.

First off, a guy who orders an apple instead of steak ain't smart enough to start a civilization. Hell, they hadn't even invented cash registers yet. What's he ordering a Granny Smith when the ribeyes was free?

Second off, judging by the way men think about vehicles, the smart money's giving twelve-to-one that man evolved from apes to Trent Lott.

See, most men think all they gotta do is get a sweet machine, and the ladies'll be flopping around 'em like a herd of gooses. Ain't so.

This ain't to say your vehicle selection don't got consequences. Fact is, for lesser trash, a decent machine is the only thing keeping you from reading *Vanity Fair*.

But them sociologists is always saying vehicles is an extension of ourselves. I don't know what that means. Which is why I got me this scientific survey.

It's for finding out what vehicles is decent and manly, and what is for guys who can get hammered on stuff made in blenders. The survey was done very scientific-like, which means we didn't do no shots till the interviewing was over.

You got a problem with that?

Pickups

Obviously, pickup trucks offer the manliest in driving experiences. Personally, ol' Verne is a Ford man. But you gotta like that Dodge Ram. It got a hood the size of a bowling alley, and it's named after an animal that head-butts stuff, which would make him a good partner for bar fighting.

But the fact is, there ain't no going wrong with a full-size pickup—unless it's made by them Japaneses, who suck at hockey, or the bed's so clean you could iron Sunday dresses on it.

That ain't true about midget pickups. According to that science I was telling you about, 98 percent of 'em is driven by fitness instructors. Seventy-two percent never caught a fish bigger than them mail-order brides from Taiwan. And 113 percent think NASCAR is a country by Egypt.

Station Wagons

The most underrated vehicle.

First off, they pass the number-one test for determining a decent White Trash machine: They can haul plywood.

Second off, they'll score you sympathy points.

Most people figure a guy driving a wagon collects ceramic cats. Either way, that makes you invisible, leaving you free to drunk drive and haul oversized loads of scrap iron.

When a cop sees a sport-utility vehicle swerving on the road, he usually says, "That man is compensating for a very small penis and is probably snorting coke. Let's pull him over, Mel."

But when a cop sees a swerving station wagon, he says, "Poor schmuck. His wife probably jacked him in the divorce and all he can afford is a goddamned station wagon. Whattaya say we let this one go, Mel?"

I once had a wagon with a rusted-out floorboard so you could dump your empties along the freeway for the bums to pick up. That's why station wagons is also good for community service.

Luxury Vehicles

A lotta people don't figure White Trash got luxury cars. But say you built yourself up a decent chop-shop business, and you're fixing to buy your woman something nice. For my money, there ain't no better machine than the Lincoln.

First off, Lincolns is named after a famous president who got a good beard, which means he could probably hunt muskrat. And let it be said that the Lincoln is the finest barhopping machine on Earth. If your pal Joey starts ralphing in the back, you can roll down the power windows from the driver's seat so's he don't get it on the carpet. It's also got a big trunk, which is good if you're gonna kidnap your ex-girlfriend's dog.

Minivans

Minivans is kind of like station wagons: They get a bad rap even though they can haul plywood.

The upside is minivans got good kid-hauling powers,

and can carry a decent amount of sawhorses or Sheetrock if you're burglarizing garages.

Problem is, 83 percent of people figure if you own a minivan, you probably shoulda just dumped the wife and kids and paid child support instead, on account of it's cheaper. Which makes you one of them fiscally irresponsibles. Which is why you shouldn't buy no goddamned minivan.

Wimp Vehicles

Wimp cars is them cigar boxes with wheels that got names like Altima or Estrogen. Most people get to figuring wimp cars is for hairdressers and environmentalists. Which they is.

They don't got good clearance when you're ditch driving and get wrecked up easy when you get hammered and hit the neighbor's garage.

However, 89 percent said if you was to put a brush guard on, even an Escort would look cool. They're also good for ramming Mercedes when you're jousting for the last parking spot at the Broncos game, on account of a crumpled hood will make 'em look manlier.

Sports Cars

Ol' Verne got a serious beef about sports cars.

Okay, so there ain't nothing finer than a babe with one of them top-shelf peroxide jobs, driving down the freeway with the wind in her big hair, looking like she got a blonde tumbleweed attached to her head.

That, friends, is good living.

But it ain't so pretty when you see Skippy, cute little executive, shoved into his red sports car from France, driving like Ernie Irvan on crank cuz he's late for his Lamaze class.

Seventy-nine percent of guys with sports cars ain't very good at softball. Eighty-one percent cross picket lines. And 163 percent would be mostly blubber and mush if you was in a plane crash and got stranded and had to eat 'em.

Sport-Utility Vehicles

These used to be the preferred vehicle of four out of five trash. "I drive through highway medians and don't gotta stop if I hit a grocery store." That was the message they sent.

Sport-utility vehicles was also good for shining deer and tearing up your girlfriend's yard after she dumped you.

But then the yuppies started buying 'em. Everything went to &%$#.

According to them sciences, 82 percent—give or take 40 percent—says sport-utility vehicles is now for lightweights. The heaviest thing they haul these days is soccer equipment and cappuccino.

Unless you gotta pre-'90s American-made with a classy naked lady hood ornament, the only thing this truck says is, "I can't change my own oil; please pass the Cafe Vienna."

(It's about time you
shut your piehole,
Verne.)

Now that you read this far—or got somebody to read it for you—you're finally realizing what it takes to live the wholesome White Trash way.

Problem is, some of you is getting them feelings of inadequacy. You know you ain't lived right. You know you been sneaking Zimas and watching *Friends* reruns with the shades drawn. And you're probably saying to yourself, "Thanks, Dr. Verne, for showing me that my life has fallen into a state of despair."

You're ready to amend your ways.

Yuppies Anonymous: A Twelve-Step Guide to Rectifying Your Sissy Ways

The good thing is that, nowadays, you get to blame this stuff on a disadvantaged childhood, which is the polite way of saying your folks sucked.

Maybe you was raised in some fruity subdivision with too many goddamned windsocks. Or maybe you wasn't privileged enough to shoot long arms out of a duck boat when you was young.

Don't worry. According to them modern sciences, going sissy, setting fire to the Junior Miss department at Kmart, or asking your grandpa's false teeth for a date to the prom, all that stuff gets blamed on disadvantaged childhoods these days. Don't ask me why. Just be thankful I'm giving you a good excuse here.

Problem is, them scientists ain't invented no dope to cure you. Which is why you need my twelve-step program, Yuppies Anonymous.

As long as you're in a twelve-step program, you get to say you're "recovering," which means chicks will have pity and won't get as mad when you paw at 'em. It offers you, the Volvo-driving fruity, the chance to do something about your sickness. I ain't saying you'll get dewussified. But at least the meetings got free coffee and lots of people to bum smokes from.

The Yuppies Anonymous Twelve-Step Tradition

1. I admit that I am powerless over brie and white wine and grinding my own coffee beans from some candy-ass place in South America nobody ever heard of, and that my life has become wussified.

2. I have come to believe that a power greater than me can restore me to sanity, so I'll stop posing in the mirror trying to look like them guys from the Bencttou ads.

3. I made the decision to turn my life over to the care of some decent White Trash, who'll drown me in a flower-pot if I even get to thinking about wearing pants that don't got no blood or paint stains on 'em.

4. I made a searching and fearless moral inventory of myself. Okay, so I lied. But I got the idea on blocks in my front yard. I should be getting to it any day now.

5. I admitted to God, myself, and another human being the exact nature of my wrongs—only I left out the part about the sixteen-year-old on that business trip to Boston. I swear she looked at least twenty-two.

6. I am entirely ready to have God remove all these defects of character, even if He's gotta torture my ass with some dental equipment from the Nazis

7. I humbly ask God to remove my shortcomings, so I can throw out them goddamned garbanzo beans and bee-line it to Old Country Buffet.

8. I made a list of all people I had harmed, and became willing to make amends to them all, except that old guy whose car I rammed at the hardware store last week. He shouldn't have parked so close.

9. I made direct amends to such people wherever

possible, except if it was at the same time the Mariners—Royals was on satellite.

10. I continued to take a personal inventory and when I was wrong admitted it, just so it wasn't about that liquor store robbery on Thirteenth Avenue last Tuesday. I got an alibi.

11. I sought through prayer, meditation, and plenty of liquor to improve my conscious contact with the White Trash, praying only for knowledge and a few extra bucks, seeing as how knowledge don't get you %$#@ if you're living in some bushes in the park.

12. Having had a spiritual awakening as a result of these steps, I tried to carry this message to other yuppies, so's they would owe me when they got cured and probably buy me beers.

Okay, so I know what you're saying right now. "Damn, Verne, this here book is what's known as your literary masterpiece, one of them staggering works of heartfelt geniuses."

Which'd be a good call on your part.

Fact is, when the *New York Times* gets to reviewing this bad boy, they're gonna start saying stuff like "tour de force" and "taut, edge-of-your-seat thriller," which is candy-ass for saying this book ain't worth buying, but probably worth stealing.

Which is why I'm not understanding how you trashes still got questions. What? You want me to write it in Braille too?

The White Zinfandel Crisis

Dear Dr. Verne:

Last weekend, on the promise of getting a Texas fifth of Jack, I helped my worthless brother-in-law replace the tranny in his candy red '72 Nova. Later that day, he came over and gave me a sixer of light beer and something called White Zinfandel (only it wasn't white, it was sissy pink).

I yelled at him, told him to never come back. Was I right to act this way? Should I have accepted the light beer and wine? I assume they got alcohol in them.

—Clyde in Bangor, Maine

Dear Clyde:

Yeah, they got alcohol in 'em, but only enough to get Ashton Kutcher hammered. And most folks say if you drink 'em, you'll go weird and start talking about Julie Andrews movies.

See, if you're in a bar and you're ordering light beer, you might as well be saying, "I enjoy wearing women's undergarments and could you please turn the big screen to soccer." I could go on about what you call your sociological implications, but the short of it is, light beer's for guys who cried during *Sleepless in Seattle*.

As for the zinfandel, it's obviously Europe-sounding, where nobody can even clean their own fish, much less do a decent Pizza Hut robbery.

I'm figuring you gotta get this guy away from your sister, before they get to reproducing. The guy probably can't even punch out a school administrator. You don't want your nephew getting no poor role modeling.

Dockers Anonymous

Dear Dr. Verne:

I think of myself as kind of a regular guy. I drive a pickup, drink domestic beer straight out of the can, wear boots, and ain't never used any of that sissy sunscreen. I got one problem: I wear Dockers trousers. Not the kind with the fruity pleats, but dang if they're still Dockers and I got to put 'em on every day. Is there a support group like Dockers Anonymous or some head shrinker that can help me?

P.S. I ain't no sissy lawyer or nothing like that.

—Mike in Billings

Dear Mike:

You keep talking about trousers and pleats, and guys from the FCC is gonna shut down my book on account of it got obscenities in it.

Now, wearing Dockers is one of the Original Sins, right up there with punching grandmas and singing along with Ashlee Simpson on the radio. I'd be damn sure I wasn't outside when it's lightning out. Three-to-one says

God smokes your ass before I get done with this here response.

See, everybody knows Dockers guys is kin to Liberace. In the commercials, they're never talking about venison sausage or Skoal or repacking the bearings on a '82 Trans Am. They're always saying dainty stuff like, "My, that's a nice blouse you got on."

I'm thinking you need medical attention. Back when I was young, if I was to ever act fruity—like maybe watch public TV—Verne Sr. would take me out back and pound my ass with a Weber grill.

This is what medical guys call your Pavlovian experience. Anytime you go fruity, like say the words "trousers" or "pleats," one of your buddies should smack you with a grill. Take it from me: A guy gets to learning fast this way, specially if it's got burning charcoals in it.

Scumbag Lawyer: "Babes Won't Listen to Me"

Dear Dr. Verne:

I need your help. I am an attorney in Orchard Park, N.Y. There are three women in my life who are making it a living hell: my secretary, who does what she wants when she wants; my colleague, who criticizes everything I do; and my wife, who only lets me have some once in a blue moon.

How can I get these women to do what I want?
—*PW'd in Orchard Park*

Dear Candy-Ass Lawyer:
In case you ain't noticed, this here book is called *White Trash Etiquette*. Which means we're supposed to be talking about power steering and drunk driving and demolition derbies. Which means we ain't supposed to be talking about sissy lawyer problems. That's what they got *Esquire* for.

Now a course no woman gonna pay you respect. You're a lawyer, for chrissakes.

Let me ask you this: Say you got a friend who got this dainty-ass job, right? And say all this guy does for a living is throw paperwork at people and wear suits made by some guy who drinks Chardonnay and thinks Beer Nuts is too fattening. Would you A.) respect him, or B.) beat him with a wood splitter?

Your secretary don't listen to you cuz she don't have to. What you gonna do about it? Hairspray her?

Same goes for the wife. Most lawyers got pipes like bankers. What you gonna say? "If you sleep with me honey, I'll show you my BlackBerry?" Just be thankful she ain't sold your ass to one of them animal testing labs.

Now about this colleague. I don't know what

the hell you're talking about, but it sounds like pervert talk. You ain't one of them creeps who collects pictures of naked children, is you?

I'm thinking you need what you call your intensive therapy. First off, you gotta quit that fruity job. On the manly scale, it's like being a theater major.

Second off, lose the cute little Tommy Hilfiger uniforms you probably wear in your off time. The only ladies that stuff attracts is them fancy ones with the smiles so tight they look like they're held up with scaffolding. Buy yourself something classy instead, like a couple of London Fletcher jerseys.

Then you gotta get manly in your talking. Me, I'd start out by practicing some basic phrases like, "Woman, you got more of that roast beef?" or "I wonder what a DNR permit costs for hunting Carrot Top."

Then you gotta trade in your briefcase for a tool belt. Since you probably still walk prissy, I'd stick something big in it just to compensate, like maybe a shop vac.

Finally, I'd weld me a winch and a blade on the front of your Nissan Pathfinder so it don't look like all you haul is them Waterford crystals. If you got no blade, just cut the metal outta your neighbor's BMW when it's dark out, then brace it with some treated four-by-fours.

She ain't gonna look pretty, but the ladies is gonna think you got more chest hairs.

My Old Man's Gone Sissy

Dear Dr. Verne:

I'm sixteen and I got a problem. It's my old man. I mean, he's cool enough, was a grunt in 'Nam and rolls his own ammo for his .44 mag.

The trouble is his job. He's a registered nurse. I got in so many fights about it in school I got expelled. I keep begging him to get a manly job, like loading trucks at the co-op or faking a back injury in a fight with a psych patient and go on disability.

But he just tells me to shut up and be glad he can afford my Ritalin. How can I deal with this, Doc?

—Ike in Minot

Dear Ike:

If the old man keeps registered nursing, sooner or later he's bound to buy a Range Rover, just so's he can get a good parking place at the Nordstrom sale. He's gonna forget how to cuss. And you'll know he's on the brink of lesbianism when he starts hyphenating his last name and trying to order them big salads at Long John Silver's.

What you gotta do is appeal to the old man's heart. Let him know that you care too much to

see him go wussified, and that if he don't quit that damn registered nursing, God'll send him to the dainty part of Hell, where they only serve Coors Light and the big screens all show figure skating.

Before we finish, let's bow our heads in some prayers for the Ten Commandments. Last thing we need is St. Peter on our ass. If someone messes up the paperwork and we get to Heaven by mistake, we could probably still borrow money from the guy.

1. You shall have no other Gods before me—except for cable TV.

2. You shall not make no carved image of Heaven above, cuz God owns the merchandising rights. Don't try horning in on His turf or He'll beat your ass with a pool cue.

3. You shall not take the Lord's name in vain, unless it involves bosses, the Los Angeles Lakers, or shooting yourself in the kidney while you're out pheasant hunting.

4. Remember the Sabbath day, keep it holy. If God wanted you to work, He would have made football on Tuesdays. Any moron knows that.

5. Honor your father and mother, cuz someday they're gonna croak. You could inherit their F-150 if you stop acting like an ingrate.

6. You shall not commit murder, except when there's a good reason, like finding your old man in bed with the cashier from the Dairy Queen.

7. You shall not commit adultery at the same motel where your sister-in-law works.

8. You shall not steal. (Only applies in Utah and France.)

9. You shall not bear false witness against your neighbor, unless you figure he's gonna rat you out on that bowling alley robbery. Then beat him to the punch.

10. You shall not covet your neighbor's house, nor shall you covet your neighbor's wife, especially if he's about to get released on parole. Then again, if he's doing time for something sissy like embezzling from a flower shop, covet all you want.

About the Author

After graduating in just eleven years from the White Trash Studies program at the University of Wisconsin—Green Bay, DR. VERNE EDSTROM, ESQ., set out to write a book Emily Post would be proud of—if she knew how to hang drywall and steer a bass boat with her feet. PETE KOTZ, a.k.a. Verne, lives in Cleveland, where he edits *Cleveland Scene,* one of the Midwest's best alternative weeklies.